M000286997

Happy Knitting!

Gina
XOXO

love!

Sleepy Eyes Knits:

Wonderlace

Knitwear Designs and Photographs by Gina House

This book is dedicated to

Sarah Taylor Selli,

the friend who test knitted (even a shawl!) for me,
nagged me, nudged me
promoted me, put up with me
and never gave up on me.

Photographs, Knitted Designs and Text Copyright © 2013 by Gina House

All rights reserved. This book or any portion thereof
may not be reproduced or used in any manner whatsoever
without the express written permission of the author.

First Printing, September 2013

Signature Book Printing, Inc.

http://www.sbpbooks.com

Printed in the United States of America
ISBN: 978-0-578-12861-0

Table of Contents

About Wonderlace

Hello Lace Knitters!

Wonderlace is a fairytale-inspired collection of knits, with lace difficulty ranging from easy to advanced. I'm so continually inspired by all of the amazing lace designers in the knitting community that I finally decided to create my own collection of lace knits to share. I **love** knitting lace *(especially during the summer months)* and I sometimes spend hours on Ravelry looking through the beautiful lace shawl designs. I've been lucky to have found (and knit!) some incredible lace patterns in the past - you know, the ones that you are always excited to show friends that you're working on and spend hours admiring your own project? Those experiences were *so heavenly*!

I hope that you find some of the designs in MY book which give you this same feeling. And, **please**, take my advice and use the VERY BEST yarn you have for these designs. It truly makes a difference in how much you will love them. The yarns that I chose for these lace patterns are some of my favorites - *either because of their texture, softness, drape or overall awesomeness*. I know that you have special yarn stashed away which you are saving for that "special project"...well, **now is the time**! Wake that yarn from its eternal slumber with a sweet needle-y kiss. I promise that you will enjoy every moment of your lace knitting experience if using a magical, wonderful yarn. ***Especially cashmere or silk.*** If you have that hidden in your sexy lingerie drawer, TAKE IT OUT! When you come back with your delicious yarn, make sure to look through the **lace difficulty** chart below. Then, *begin, my sweet!*

Happy Knitting! *Love, Gina*

Lace Difficulty *(the number of yarn balls indicates how challenging it is)* will be indicated by a colored ball of yarn:

- *Advanced Beginner* (1 yarn ball, simple design, easy to understand lace pattern, knit flat)
- *Advanced Beginner/Intermediate* (2 yarn balls, may include more than one lace pattern, knitted in the round, more complex lace)
- *Intermediate* (3 yarn balls, shaping, may include add-on items to attach, more complex lace)
- *Intermediate/Challenging* (4 yarn balls, intricate lace, more than one lace pattern/chart, requires detailed blocking)

Gauge & Abbreviations

Why is gauge so important?

Have you ever knit a sweater and, after months of hopeful hours knitting, you tried it on and it didn't fit? Either it's too big, too small, the arms are too long or it ended up being a crop top instead of a full length sweater? Or perhaps you knit a beautiful hat and then you realize it comes down over your eyes or, even worse, it won't fit over your head?

This is why gauge is **so** important.

Every knitter is unique and special. So, it makes sense that our knitting styles and tensions may be unique as well.

Taking time to <u>knit a 4"/20 cm square</u> before knitting the actual project is not only helpful for size, but it also gives you an idea of how your knitted item will drape, look and feel. You may decide that you *LOVE* the yarn you're using. More often than not, you will look at the swatch and think, *"Hmmm...not really loving it"*. Then, you have time to change the yarn to one that you *are* happy with. Instead of wearing a hand knit sweater that you have regrets about, you will be wearing one you are **proud** and **excited** to wear.

Gauge swatches make ALL the difference!

Please **make a gauge swatch** and **read through each pattern carefully and fully** before beginning each project. You'll be happy you did. *Promise!*

BO	bind off
CC1	contrast color 1
CC2	contrast color 2
CO	cast on
CS	center stitch
k	knit
k2tog	knit 2 sts together at the same time
k3tog	knit 3 sts together at the same time
k3togtbl	knit 3 sts together at the same time, through the back loop
LN	left needle
m1	make one st, your choice
m1L	pick up yarn between 2 sts with LN from front to back, knit into the back of the st
m1R	pick up yarn between 2 sts with LN from back to front, knit into the front of the st
m1p	make 1 st purlwise
MC	main color
n, N	needle: dpn, Magic Loop/2 Circs
p	purl
p2tog	purl 2 sts together at the same time
p2togtbl	purl 2 sts together through the back loop
PM	place marker
RN	right needle
rs	right side
s2kp	slip 2 sts at the same time knitwise, knit 1 st, then pass both slipped sts over the knit st
sk2p	slip 1 st knitwise, knit 2 sts together, then pass the slipped st over the knit 2 together
sl1	slip 1 st purlwise
skp	slip 1 st knitwise, k 1 st, pass the slipped st over
SM	slip marker
ssk	slip 2 sts knitwise, one at a time, then knit both through the back loop
st(s)	stitch(es)
ws	wrong side
yo	yarn over

Poison Apple Beret

This feminine, lacy beret is knit using a luxurious yarn of silk and mohair with an alluring drape. The lovely character of **Snow White** was the inspiration for this lightweight, but also surprisingly warm beret. It's extremely flattering on all types of head shapes and looks beautiful in all colors.

Pattern Difficulty:

Yarn:
(1) 2.8 oz/80 g skein (400 yds/365.8 m) of **Artyarns** *Rhapsody Light* (50% silk/50% kid mohair) in "H7".

(Only **231yds/211.2 m** or 1.5 oz/45 g are used for hat.)

Yarn Substitute:
(1) 1.76 oz/50 g skein (440 yds/402.3 m) of **Knit Picks** *Gloss Lace* (70% Merino Wool/30% silk) in "24245 fiesta" and
(1) 0.88 oz/25 g skein (246 yds/224.9 m) of **Knit Picks** *Aloft* (75% super kid mohair/25% silk) in "25204 cranberry".

(In this version, both yarns are held at the same time while knitting. This combination makes a bit larger and deeper hat. I would recommend omitting one repeat of the lace pattern if using this combination - unless you like a very deep hat or have very thick hair.)

Needle: US 3 (3 mm) 16"/40.6 cm circular and a set of dpns in the same size or needle size necessary to obtain gauge

Gauge: 8 sts and **10** rows = 1"/2.5 cm (stockinette)

Notions: 15 small stitch markers *(1 of one color and 14 of another color)*, scissors, tapestry needle, row counter, measuring tape

Finished Size: Women's medium/large for **21-23"**/53.3 - 58.4 cm head circumference

Note: A deeper beret can be made by adding another full repeat of the lace pattern. *(Each lace pattern repeat measures around **2"**/5 cm in height.)*

Directions

CO **120** sts.

1. Ribbing:

Round 1: (k1, p1) across round
Repeat Round 1 for **1"**/2.5 cm

2. Increase Section:

(k2, m1) across round = **180 sts** total

3. Body of Hat:

Purl 1 round. (**NOTE:** On the next round, you'll be adding a stitch marker every **12 sts**.)

Knit 1 round.

Follow the **Smiling Diamonds Lace** pattern for approx. **6"**/ 15.2 cm or **3** full repeats *(60 rounds)*.

Purl 1 round, removing st markers as you go along.

4. Decrease Section: (**NOTE** - you will be <u>moving the beginning of round st on every odd round</u>.)

Round 1: k10, s2kp, k1, PM, *k8, s2kp, k1, PM*; repeat *...* 14 times total, k8, sl2 sts purlwise to RN, remove stitch marker (m), place 2 sts from LN to RN, PM back on LN *(This marker is the beginning of the round marker and should be a different color than the other stitch markers.)*, move 4 sts back to LN, s2kp, k1.

Round 2 and every even round: knit

Round 3: k7, s2kp, remove m, k1, replace m, SM, *k6, s2kp, remove m, k1, replace m, SM*; repeat *...* to end of round.

Round 5: k5, s2kp, remove m, k1, replace m, SM, *k4, s2kp, remove m, k1, replace m, SM*; repeat *...* to end of round.

Round 7: k3, s2kp, remove m, k1, replace m, SM, *k2, s2kp, remove m, k1, replace m, SM*; repeat *...* to end of round.

Round 9: k1, s2kp, remove m, k1, replace m, SM, *s2kp, remove m, k1, replace m, SM*; repeat *...* to end of round.

Round 10: knit around, removing markers

Round 11: k2tog around

Round 12: knit (*16 total sts*)

Cut yarn, leaving a **10-12"/**25.4 - 30.5 cm tail, thread onto a tapestry needle and thread through all sts and pull tight. Knot on the inside of the hat.

5. Finishing:

Weave in all ends, neatly. You may wish to lightly steam the beret (*under a press cloth and using a tailor's ham*) to open up the lace a bit.

Smiling Diamonds Lace: (*12 stitch repeat*)

Round 1: *yo, ssk, k7, k2tog, yo, k1*; repeat *...* around

Round 2 and all even rounds: knit

Round 3: *k1, yo, ssk, k5, k2tog, yo, k2*; repeat *...* around

Round 5: *(yo, ssk)2x, k3, (k2tog, yo)2x, k1; repeat *...* around

Round 7: *k1, (yo, ssk)2x, k1, (k2tog, yo)2x, k2*; repeat *...* around

Round 9: *(yo, ssk)2x, yo, sk2p, yo, (k2tog, yo)2x, k1*; repeat *...* around

Round 11: *k3, k2tog, yo, k1, yo, ssk, k4*; repeat *...* around

Round 13: *k2, k2tog, yo, k3, yo, ssk, k3*; repeat *...* around

Round 15: *k1, (k2tog, yo)2x, k1, (yo, ssk)2x, k2*; repeat *...* around

Round 17: *(k2tog, yo)2x, k3, (yo, ssk)2x, k1*; repeat *...* around

Round 19: k1, *(k2tog, yo)2x, k1, (yo, ssk)2x, yo, sk2p, yo*; repeat *...* to last 11 sts, (k2tog, yo)2x, k1, (yo, ssk)2x, yo, slip 2 sts pw to RN, remove st marker, move st from LN over to RN, replace st marker back onto LN, place 3 sts back onto LN, sk2p, yo.

Round 20: m1, knit the rest of the round

Repeat Rounds 1-20 for pattern.

Key

☐	Knit	k
	(RS) Knit (WS) Purl	
⬧ (K1 tbl symbol)	K1 tbl	k1 tbl
	(RS) knit 1 stitch through back loop	
╱	Knit 2 Together	k2tog
	(RS) Knit 2 stitches together	
⅄	Knit 3 Together	k3tog
	(RS) Knit 3 stitches together	
⅄	Knit 3 Together Tbl	k3tog tbl
	(RS) Knit 3 stitches together through back loop	
Ⓜ	Make One Knitwise	m1
	(RS) Make one by lifting strand in between stitch just worked and the next stitch, knit into back of this thread	
Ⓜ	Make One Purlwise	m1p
	(RS) Make one by lifting strand in between stitch just worked and the next stitch, purl into back of this thread	
•	Purl	p
	(RS) Purl (WS) Knit	
╱•	Purl 2 Together	p2tog
	(RS) Purl 2 Together	
╲•	Purl 2 Together Tbl	p2tog tbl
	(RS) Purl 2 stitches together through back loop	
✕	Sl2 Kwise K1 Psso	s2kp
	(RS) slip 2 sts knitwise, k1, pass the slipped sts over	
③	SK2P	sk2p
	(RS) Slip K2tog PSSO	
△	Slip Knit Pass Over	skp
	(RS) Slip 1, knit 1, pass slipped stitch over	
⩔	Slip With Yarn In Back	slip wyib
	(RS) yarn in back (WS) Slip stitch as if to purl, holding yarn in the front	
╲	Slip Slip Knit	ssk
	(RS) slip, slip, knit slipped sts together	
■	No Stitch	x
	(RS) No Stitch (WS) No Stitch	
Ⓞ	Yarn Over	yo
	(RS) Yarn Over	

Smiling Diamonds Lace

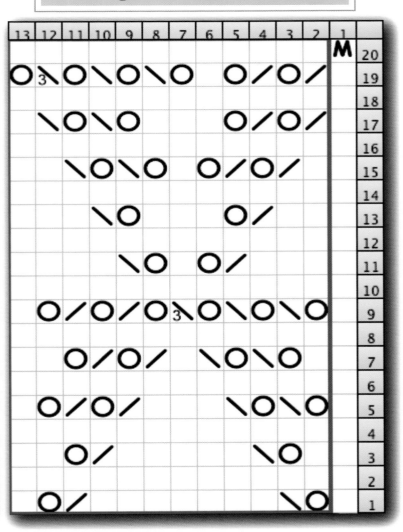

Repeat pattern in **BLUE.**

9

Loralee Cowl

This beautifully soft, double length cowl pattern is knit in the round from the bottom up. It can be worn in various ways, such as a fully open circle scarf around the neck, doubled up on itself as a close-to-the-neck cowl and even around the neck and then over the top of the head as a snood. This pattern is designed with two beginner lace patterns alternated with garter stitch and finished with an optional crocheted edging, which provides extra stability. For a more unisex version, you can substitute the lace sections with stockinette or seed stitch (for a warmer and more textured option).

Pattern Difficulty:

Yarn:
(4) 1.76 oz/50 g skeins (100 yds/91.4 m) of **Classic Elite**
   Waterlily (100% merino wool) in "apricot #1950" OR
400 yards/365.8 m or 3.52 oz/100 g of worsted weight, kettle
dyed 100% merino wool.

Needle: US **8** (5 mm), 32"/81.3 cm circular needle or needle
size necessary to obtain gauge

Hook: US **H** (5 mm) *(optional)*

Gauge: **4** sts and **8** rows = 1"/2.5 cm (garter)

Notions: tapestry needle, stitch markers, scissors, measuring
tape

Finished Size: **26"** x **8"**/66 cm wide x 20.3 cm tall

Directions

1. Body of Cowl:

Being careful not to twist, **CO 198 sts** and join in the round.
Place a marker to indicate the beginning of the round.

Follow the **Garter Stitch** pattern for 0.5"/1.27 cm (or **4
rounds**) -

Purl 1 round.
Knit 1 round.
Purl 1 round.
Knit 1 round.

Follow the **Crescent Lace** pattern for **8 rounds** (2 repeats).

Follow the **Chinese Fan** lace pattern for **24 rounds** (2
repeats).

Purl 2 rounds.

Follow the **Crescent Lace** pattern for **8 rounds** (2 repeats).

Follow the **Garter Stitch** pattern for 0.5"/1.27 cm (or **4
rounds**).

BO all stitches. *See below for optional crochet edging or cut
yarn and pull through last stitch to secure. Weave in all ends.

2. Optional Crocheted Edging*:

Instead of cutting the yarn and pulling through the last stitch,
place your crochet hook into the last stitch and begin the
Herringbone Half Double Crochet stitch around the entire
circumference of the bottom edge on *EVERY OTHER* stitch.

Cut yarn, leaving a 3"/7.6 cm tail and secure. Follow the exact same process for the top edge of the cowl, using your crochet hook and remaining yarn to pull a loop through one of the stitches to begin.

Herringbone Half Double Crochet:

Yo, insert hook into the next indicated stitch, yo, bring the yarn through the stitch AND the leftmost (or first) loop on the hook, yo, bring the yarn through BOTH loops on the hook.

Repeat from *...* *(remember: follow these instructions on **every other** stitch!)*

3. Finishing:

Block lightly: either by soaking in wool wash, squeezing out excess water and drying flat OR gently steaming the cowl under a cotton press cloth using an iron and laying flat to dry.

Crescent Lace: *(7+ 2 stitch repeat)*

Round 1: k1, *k1, k2tog, yo, k1, yo, ssk, k1; repeat from * to last st, k1
Round 2 & 4: knit
Round 3: k1, *k2tog, yo, k3, yo, ssk; repeat from * to last st, k1

Repeat Rounds 1-4 for pattern.

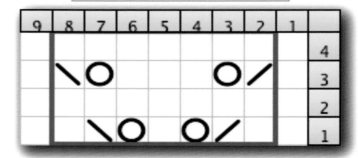

Crescent Lace

Repeat pattern in **BLUE.**

Key			
Knit k (RS) Knit (WS) Purl		Purl 2 Together Tbl p2tog tbl (RS) Purl 2 stitches together through back loop	
K1 tbl k1 tbl (RS) knit 1 stitch through back loop		Sl2 Kwise K1 Psso s2kp (RS) slip 2 sts knitwise, k1, pass the slipped sts over	
Knit 2 Together k2tog (RS) Knit 2 stitches together		SK2P sk2p (RS) Slip K2tog PSSO	
Knit 3 Together k3tog (RS) Knit 3 stitches together		Slip Knit Pass Over skp (RS) Slip 1, knit 1, pass slipped stitch over	
Knit 3 Together Tbl k3tog tbl (RS) knit 3 stitches together through back loop		Slip With Yarn In Back slip wyib (RS) yarn in back (WS) Slip stitch as if to purl, holding yarn in the front	
Make One Knitwise m1 (RS) Make one by lifting strand in between stitch just worked and the next stitch, knit into back of this thread		Slip Slip Knit ssk (RS) slip, slip, knit slipped sts together	
Make One Purlwise m1p (RS) Make one by lifting strand in between stitch just worked and the next stitch, purl into back of this thread		No Stitch x (RS) No Stitch (WS) No Stitch	
Purl p (RS) Purl (WS) Knit		Yarn Over yo (RS) Yarn Over	
Purl 2 Together p2tog (RS) Purl 2 Together			

Chinese Fan Lace: *(9 stitch repeat)*

Round 1: purl
Round 2: purl
Round 3: *ssk, yo, k1, yo, k4, k2tog; repeat from * across round
Rounds 4, 6, 8, 10, 12: knit
Round 5: *ssk, (k1, yo)2x, k3, k2tog; repeat from * across round
Round 7: *ssk, k2, yo, k1, yo, k2, k2tog; repeat from * across round
Round 9: *ssk, k3, (yo, k1)2x, k2tog; repeat from * across round
Round 11: *ssk, k4, yo, k1, yo, k2tog; repeat from * across round
Round 12: purl

Repeat Rounds 1-12 for pattern.

Chinese Fan Lace

9	8	7	6	5	4	3	2	1	
									12
/	O		O					\	11
									10
/		O		O				\	9
									8
/			O		O			\	7
									6
/				O		O		\	5
									4
/					O		O	\	3
•	•	•	•	•	•	•	•	•	2
•	•	•	•	•	•	•	•	•	1

Repeat pattern in **BLUE.**

Beauty Shawl

This airy, feminine and flowing shawl was inspired by Belle's ball gown in "*Beauty & the Beast*". I loved watching how the dress moved while she danced and the bright, cheerful color. This 3/4 crescent shaped, chevron lace shawl is knit in 5 consecutive wedge sections and ends with an increasing fan stitch for a sweet, ruffly edge.

Pattern Difficulty:

Yarn:

MC - (1) 1.76 oz/50 g skein (440 yds/402 m) of **Knit Picks** *Shadow Tonal* (100% merino wool) in "gold"

CC - (1) 1 lb/453.6 g cone (5040 yds/4609 m) cone of **Jaggerspun** *Zephyr Wool/Silk* (50% wool, 50% silk) in "white" *(882 yds/806.5 m used in pattern)*

CC2 - (1) 3 oz/85 g skein (498 yds/455 m) of **Patons** *Lace* (80% acrylic, 10% mohair, 10% wool) in "vintage antique" *(125 yds/ 114.3 m used in pattern)*

OR approximately **1,447 yards**/1,322 m of a 2 ply laceweight yarn.

Needle: US **5** (3.75 mm) and US **7** (4.5 mm) *(for binding off)* in either a 32-47"/81.3-119.4 cm circular needle or needle size necessary to obtain gauge

Gauge: **7** sts and **9** rows = 1"/2.5 cm (stockinette)

Notions: 6 stitch markers *(2 of one color for garter edges and 4 of another color)*, 4 clip on stitch markers *(or small safety pins)*, scissors, tapestry needle, row counter *(or pen & paper)*, blocking wires and pins, waste yarn/dental floss in a contrasting color for provisional cast on and for making a lifeline *(optional)*, 700 seed beads *(optional, see page 17)***

Finished Size: 23" x 84"/58.4 cm x 213.4 cm (measured from neck to bottom edge and then along the bottom of the ruffled edge) *(blocked)*

Directions

1. Garter Stitch Tab:

With a contrasting color waste yarn and smaller needle size, CO **2** sts.

Rows 1-4: knit
Row 5: using **MC** yarn, k2
Rows 6-10: knit
Row 11: k2, pick up and knit 1 st in each of the three garter ridges along the side of the tab. Knit the last 2 sts from the waste yarn, cutting the waste yarn as you go. *(7 sts)*

2. Shawl Set up:

Increase Rows:

The **TWO STITCHES** *at the beginning and end of the row will be* <u>garter stitch edges</u>. *Slip stitch markers as you go along.*

Set up row: (sl1, k1), PM, p3, PM, k2 *(7 sts)*
Row 1 (rs): (sl1, k1), m1L, k to last 2 sts, m1R, k2 *(9 sts)*
Row 2: (sl1, k1), purl to last 2 sts, k2

On the following row, add a clip-on stitch marker *(or safety pin)* onto each center stitch - [**CS**]. *(See **Figure A**)*

Row 3: (sl1, k1), (m1L, k1 [**CS**], m1R)5x, k2 *(19 sts)*
*As you knit additional rows, move the clip-on stitch markers to the new [**CS**] above. At some point, you will probably be able to tell where the center stitch is and you can remove these markers, if desired. From here on, you will be slipping the stitch markers at the beginning and end of each row, next to the garter edges.*

Row 4 and all ws rows: (sl1, k1), purl to the last 2 sts, k2
Row 5: (sl1, k1), (k1, m1L, k1[**CS**], m1R, k1)4x while placing a marker after each repeat, (k1, m1L, k1[**CS**], m1R, k1), k2 *(29 sts)*
Row 7: (sl1, k1), (k2, m1L, k1[**CS**], m1R, k2)5x, k2 *(39 sts)*
Row 9: (sl1, k1), (k3, m1L, k1[**CS**], m1R, k3)5x, k2 *(49 sts)*
Row 11: (sl1, k1), (k4, m1L, k1[**CS**], m1R, k4)5x, k2 *(59 sts)*
Row 13: (sl1, k1), (k5, m1L, k1[**CS**], m1R, k5)5x, k2 *(69 sts)*
Row 15: (sl1, k1), (k6, m1L, k1[**CS**], m1R, k6)5x, k2 *(79 sts)*
Row 17: (sl1, k1), (k7, m1L, k1[**CS**], m1R, k7)5x, k2 *(89 sts)*
Row 19: (sl1, k1), (k8, m1L, k1[**CS**], m1R, k8)5x, k2 *(99 sts)*
Row 21: (sl1, k1), (k9, m1L, k1[**CS**], m1R, k9)5x, k2 *(109 sts)*
Row 22: (sl1, k1), purl to last 2 sts, k2 *(109 sts)*

3. Body of the Shawl, Part A - Pretty Lace Chevron pattern:* (CHEAT SHEET available...look to next page)

Row 1 *(rs)*: (sl1, k1), {follow the **Pretty Lace Chevron** pattern/chart to [**CS**], m1L, k1 [**CS**], m1R, follow the **Pretty Lace Chevron** pattern/chart}5x, to last 2 sts, k2
Row 2 *(ws)*: (sl1, k1), purl to last 2 sts, k2

*NOTE: every RS row will **add 10 sts** along the length the shawl. After the first Row of this pattern, you will have **119 stitches**.*

Row 3: (sl1, k1), {follow the **Pretty Lace Chevron** pattern/chart over a multiple of 10 sts, knit to [**CS**], m1L, k1 [**CS**], m1R, knit to a multiple of 10 sts before next stitch marker and then follow the **Pretty Lace Chevron pattern**/chart}5x, to last 2 sts, k2
Row 4: (sl1, k1), purl to last 2 sts, k2 *(129 sts)*

Repeat **Rows 3** and **4** until you have completed the **Pretty Lace Chevron** pattern **5 times total**...ending having finished **Row 13**. Keep careful track of what row you are on for the pattern as you progress.

You will end up adding another full repeat of the **Pretty Lace Chevron** pattern on **Rows 7 and 13, AFTER** completing the first full repeat of the **Pretty Lace Chevron** pattern. At the end of the first full repeat of the **Pretty Lace Chevron** pattern *(Rows 1-14, **Figures B & C**)*, you will have **179 sts**.

For the last and final repeat (**6th** *repeat*) of the **Pretty Lace Chevron** pattern, follow the pattern/chart until **Row 5** *(change yarn to **CC1** on **Row 6** if desired OR when beginning the Ruffle Feather and Fan pattern section, your choice entirely)*, otherwise continue on with **MC**. Finish with **Row 13**. *(529 sts)*

*NOTE: After Row 11, there are 25 pattern repeats across...**50 total** Pretty Lace Chevrons across the row.*

*On **Row 14:*** (sl1, k1), purl to last 2 sts, k2 *(removing st markers as you go along)*

Set up Row 1: (sl1, k1), k1, m1L, k261, m1L, k262, m1R, k3
Set up Row 2: (sl1, k1), purl to last 2 stitches, k2 *(532 sts)*

4. Edging of Shawl, Part B - Ruffle Feather and Fan pattern: (33 repeats across on first row)

Row 1 *(rs)*: (sl1, k1), follow the **Ruffle Feather and Fan** pattern over 16 sts *(to begin with)* to last 2 sts, k2
Row 2 *(ws)*: (sl1, k1), purl across to last 2 sts, k2

Repeat Rows 1 and 2 until **Row 36**. On **Row 37**, double up the **CC1** yarn or use a third yarn (**CC2**) for the last 5 rows and bind off with **larger needle size**, using **K2TBL** method.

5. Finishing:

Block the shawl using blocking wires or blocking pins and a flat, cushiony surface *(carpet, bed, blocking squares)*. Weave in all ends.

Pretty Lace Chevron: *(10 stitch repeat)*

Row 1 *(rs)*: *yo, ssk, k2tog, yo, k1; repeat *... * to end
Row 2 *(ws)* **and all even rows:** purl
Row 3: *k1, yo, ssk, k3, k2tog, yo, k2; repeat *...* to end
Row 5: *k2, yo, ssk, k1, k2tog, yo, k3; repeat *... * to end
Row 7: *k3, yo, sk2p, yo, k4; repeat *... * to end
Rows 9, 11 and 13: *ssk, k2, yo, k1, yo, k2, k2tog, k1; repeat *... * to end
Row 14: purl

Repeat Rows 1-14 for pattern.

*To make knitting the body of the shawl (**Pretty Lace Chevron** section) easier, I have created a *"CHEAT SHEET"* that you can download from my website:

http://www.ginahouse.net/Gina_House/
Pattern_Downloads.html

Beads! You can add beads to the Pretty Lace Chevron section of the shawl on every Row 9, 11 and 13 on stitch 5 *(the k st between the yarn overs)*. This means on every 4 rows (on the WHITE rows) of the cheat sheet. The beads can be placed on each <u>center stitch</u>, on the <u>second st from the beginning</u> and on the <u>next to last st</u>. Please check out **Jessica/Patchworkgirl's Ravelry page for pictures and suggestions!

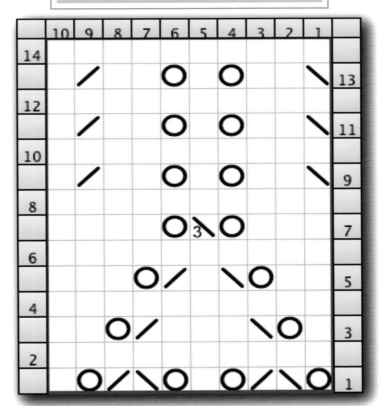

Repeat pattern in **BLUE.**

K2TBL Bind Off method:

Knit the first stitch, *knit a st, place the stitches from the right hand needle to the left hand needle, knit the next two stitches together through the back loop*. *Repeat from *...* for each stitch until all stitches are bound off.*

Key

Knit		Purl 2 Together Tbl	
k		p2tog tbl	
(RS) Knit		(RS) Purl 2 stitches together through back	
(WS) Purl		loop	
K1 tbl		Sl2 Kwise K1 Psso	
k1 tbl		s2kp	
(RS) knit 1 stitch through back loop		(RS) slip 2 sts knitwise, k1, pass the slipped sts over	
Knit 2 Together		SK2P	
k2tog		sk2p	
(RS) Knit 2 stitches together		(RS) Slip K2tog PSSO	
Knit 3 Together		Slip Knit Pass Over	
k3tog		skp	
(RS) Knit 3 stitches together		(RS) Slip 1, knit 1, pass slipped stitch over	
Knit 3 Together Tbl		Slip With Yarn In Back	
k3tog tbl		slip wyib	
(RS) knit 3 stitches together through back loop		(RS) yarn in back	
		(WS) Slip stitch as if to purl, holding yarn in the front	
Make One Knitwise		Slip Slip Knit	
m1		ssk	
(RS) Make one by lifting strand in between stitch just worked and the next stitch, knit into back of this thread		(RS) slip, slip, knit slipped sts together	
Make One Purlwise		No Stitch	
m1p		x	
(RS) Make one by lifting strand in between stitch just worked and the next stitch, purl into back of this thread		(RS) No Stitch	
		(WS) No Stitch	
Purl		Yarn Over	
p		yo	
(RS) Purl		(RS) Yarn Over	
(WS) Knit			
Purl 2 Together			
p2tog			
(RS) Purl 2 Together			

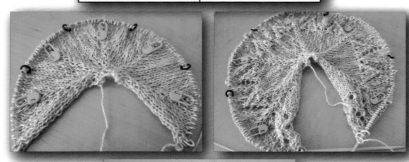

Figure A   **Figure B**

Figure C

Ruffle Feather and Fan Pattern: (beginning with a multiple of 16 stitches)

Row 1 (rs): knit

Row 2 *(ws)* **and all even rows:** purl

Rows 3 and 5: *k1, yo, s2kp yo, k1; repeat from * to end

Row 7: *k2, yo, ssk, yo, k2, yo, s2kp, yo, k2, yo, k2tog, yo, k3; repeat from * to end

Row 9: knit

Row 11: *(yo, k1)2x, yo, k3, ssk, s2kp, k2tog, k3, (yo, k1)3x; repeat from * to end

Row 13: knit

Row 15: *(yo, k1)4x, (ssk)2x, s2kp, (k2tog)2x, k1, (yo, k1)4x; repeat from * to end

Row 17: knit

Row 19: *(yo, k1)5x, (ssk)2x, s2kp, (k2tog)2x, k1, (yo, k1)5x; repeat from * to end

Row 21: knit

Row 23: *(yo, k1)5x, yo, (ssk)3x, s2kp, (k2tog)3x, (yo, k1)6x; repeat from * to end

Row 25: knit

Row 27: *(yo, k1)5x, yo, k2, (ssk)3x, s2kp, (k2tog)3x, k2, (yo, k1)6x; repeat from * to end

Row 29: knit

Row 31: *(yo, k1)7x, (ssk)4x, s2kp, (k2tog)4x, k1, (yo, k1)7x; repeat from * to end

Row 33: knit

Row 35: *(yo, k1)6x, yo, k3, (ssk)4x, s2kp, (k2tog)4x, k3, (yo, k1)7x; repeat from * to end

Row 37: knit

Row 39: *M1p, p10, M1p, p11; repeat from * to end

Row 41: purl

Ruffle Feather and Fan

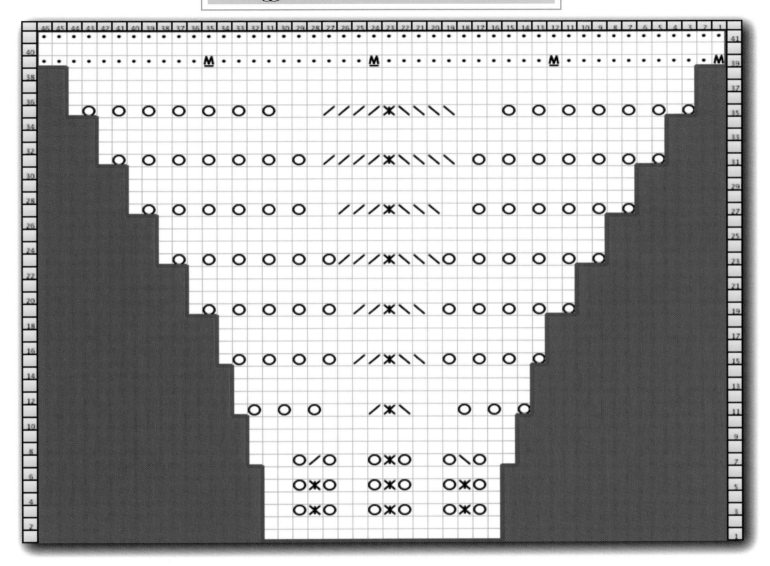

Repeat pattern in **BLUE.**

21

Queen's Mirror Shawl

*Inspired by "**Snow White & the Seven Dwarves**", this shawl incorporates lace and ripples to mimic the movement of the shimmering mirror in which the Evil Queen communicates. The bottom of the shawl features goblets (of magical transformation potion) and has a contrasting white trim to represent the standing collar of the Evil Queen's cape. This shawl pattern also offers an alternate chart for the queen's mirror, which would look stunning knitted with a vibrant purple, red or gold yarn.*

Pattern Difficulty:

Yarn:
(2) 4 oz/113.4 g skeins (420 yards/384 m) of **Mad Color**
Classica (80% Merino, 20% Nylon) in "Margharitaville"

0.42 oz/12 g partial skein (105 yds/96 m) of **Alpaca with a
Twist** *Fino* (70% Alpaca, 30% Silk) in "First Frost"

Needle: US **6** (4 mm) and **8** (5 mm), 24-32"/60.9-81.3 cm circular
or needle size necessary to obtain gauge

Gauge: *(using the smaller needle size and fingering yarn)* **6.5** sts and **7**
rows = 1"/2.5 cm (stockinette)

Notions: tapestry needle, row counter *(or pencil/paper)*, clip on
stitch marker, 22 small stitch markers, blocking pins/blocking
wires, measuring tape, scissors

Finished Size: 24" x **56"**/60.9 x 142.2 cm *(unblocked)*, **34"** x
74"/86.4 x 188 cm *(blocked)*

Note: At the very least, I recommend placing stitch markers
<u>after</u> the first 3 sts *(garter edges)*, <u>on either side of the center stitch</u>
(CS), and <u>before</u> the last 3 sts *(garter edges)*. Please feel free to
place more markers between pattern repeats throughout the
pattern. Threading a "lifeline" through all the stitches of your
shawl after every 10 rows or after each full repeat of a pattern
can be a lifesaver. If something freaky happens as you're
knitting your shawl, you'll know that you can rip back your
knitting to the last place everything was correct and start again.
I recommend using either a contrasting colored yarn in a
similar weight or dental floss. Using a tapestry needle, bring
the yarn/floss through every single stitch in the row, being very
careful not to miss any. Try to secure the ends to the shawl, to
keep the lifeline from pulling out easily.

Directions

1. Garter Stitch Tab:

Using the larger needle size, cast on **3** sts using the *backward loop
cast on*.

Switch to the smaller needle size. Work **6 rows of garter
stitch**. Do not turn your work. Rotate the tab 90 degrees then
pick up and knit 3 sts along the side of the tab *(picking the
stitches up in the garter ridges)*, rotate the tab another 90 degrees
and pick up the last **3 sts** from the cast on edge.

When the **Garter Stitch Tab** is complete, you will have *9 sts
total*.

2. Beginning Ripple Lace Pattern:

Starting row *(ws)*: (sl1, k2), purl to the last 3 sts, k3
Row 1 *(rs)*: (sl1, k2), yo, k1, yo, k1 (this is the **CENTER
STITCH – CS**...*you may wish to **add a clip on marker** to this
stitch and move it up as needed*), yo, k1, yo, k3
Row 2 *(ws)* **and all even rows:** (sl1, k2), purl to the **CS**,
k1tbl, purl to the last 3 sts, k3
Row 3: (sl1, k2), yo, k3, yo, k1 (**CS**), yo, k3, yo, k3
Row 5: (sl1, k2), yo, k5, yo, k1 (**CS**), yo, k5, yo, k3

Ending Row 6 of the **Beginning Ripple Lace** with *21 sts
total*. *(7 sts between CS and the garter stitch edges on each side).*

Row 7: (sl1, k2), *yo, k2, yo, sk2p, yo, k2, yo*, k1 (**CS**), repeat *
*, end with k3
Row 9: (sl1, k2), *yo, k1, yo, ssk, k3, k2tog, yo, k1, yo*, k1 (**CS**),
repeat * *, end with k3
Row 11: (sl1, k2), *yo, k1, yo, ssk, yo, ssk, k1, k2tog, yo, k2tog,
yo, k1, yo*, k1 (**CS**), repeat * *, end with k3

Row 13: (sl1, k2), *yo, k3, yo, ssk, yo, sk2p, yo, k2tog, yo, k3, yo*, k1(**CS**), repeat * *, end with k3

Row 15: (sl1, k2), *yo, k5, yo, ssk, k1, k2tog, yo, k5, yo*, k1(**CS**), repeat * *, end with k3

Row 17: (sl1, k2), *yo, k1, k2tog, yo, k1, yo, ssk, k1, yo, sk2p, yo, k1, k2tog, yo, k1, yo, ssk, k1, yo*, k1 (**CS**), repeat * *, end with k3

Ending Row 18 of the **Beginning Ripple Lace** with *45 sts total*.
(19 sts between the CS and garter stitch edges on each side).

Work the 20 rows of the **Main Ripple Lace** pattern below.

3. Main Ripple Lace Pattern:

Row 1 *(rs)*: (sl1, k2), yo, k1, k2tog, yo, k2, *k1, yo, ssk, k3, k2tog, yo, k2*, repeat *...* until 4 sts before **CS**, k1, yo, ssk, k1, yo, k1 (**CS**), yo, k1, k2tog, yo, k2, repeat *...* until 7 sts before end, k1, yo, ssk, k1, yo, k3

Row 2 *(ws)* **and all even rows:** (sl1, k2), p to **CS**, k1tbl, p to last 3 sts, k3

Row 3: (sl1, k2), yo, k1, (k2tog, yo)2x, k1, *(yo, ssk)2x, k1, (k2tog, yo)2x, k1*, repeat *...* until 5 sts before **CS**, (yo, ssk)2x, k1, yo, k1 (**CS**), yo, k1, (k2tog, yo)2x, k1, repeat *...* until 8 sts before end, (yo, ssk)2x, k1, yo, k3

Row 5: (sl1, k2), yo, k1, (k2tog, yo)2x, k2, *k1, yo, ssk, yo, sk2p, yo, k2tog, yo, k2*, repeat *...* until 6 sts before **CS**, k1, (yo, ssk)2x, k1, yo, k1 (**CS**), yo, k1, (k2tog, yo)2x, k2, repeat *...* until 9 sts before end, k1, (yo, ssk)2x, k1, yo, k3

Row 7: (sl1, k2), yo, k3, k2tog, yo, k3, *k2, yo, ssk, k1, k2tog, yo, k3*, repeat *...* until 7 sts before **CS**, k2, yo, ssk, k3, yo, k1 (**CS**), yo, k3, k2tog, yo, k3, repeat *...* until 10 sts, k2, yo, ssk, k3, yo, k3

Row 9: (sl1, k2), yo, k2, yo, sk2p, yo, k1, k2tog, yo, k1, *yo, ssk, k1, yo, sk2p, yo, k1, k2tog, yo, k1*, repeat *...* until 8 sts before

CS, yo, ssk, k1, yo, sk2p, yo, k2, yo, k1 (**CS**), yo, k2, yo, sk2p, yo, k1, k2tog, yo, k1, repeat *...* until 11 sts before end, yo, ssk, k1, yo, sk2p, yo, k2, yo, k3

Row 11: (sl1, k2), yo, k1, yo, ssk, k3, k2tog, yo, k2, *k1, yo, ssk, k3, k2tog, yo, k2*, repeat *...* until 9 sts before **CS**, k1, yo, ssk, k3, k2tog, yo, k1, yo, k1 (**CS**), yo, k1, yo, ssk, k3, k2tog, yo, k2, repeat *...* until 12 sts before end, k1, yo, ssk, k3, k2tog, yo, k1, yo, k3

Row 13: (sl1, k2), yo, k1, (yo, ssk)2x, k1, (k2tog, yo)2x, k1, *(yo, ssk)2x, k1, (k2tog, yo)2x, k1*, repeat *...* until 10 sts before **CS**, (yo, ssk)2x, k1, (k2tog, yo)2x, k1, yo, k1 (**CS**), yo, k1, (yo, ssk)2x, k1, (k2tog, yo)2x, k1, repeat *...* until 13 sts before end, (yo, ssk)2x, k1, (k2tog, yo)2x, k1, yo, k3

Row 15: (sl1, k2), yo, k3, yo, ssk, yo, sk2p, yo, k2tog, yo, k2, *k1, yo, ssk, yo, sk2p, yo, k2tog, yo, k2*, repeat *...* until 11 sts **CS**, k1, yo, ssk, yo, sk2p, yo, k2tog, yo, k3, yo, k1 (**CS**), yo, k3, yo, ssk, yo, sk2p, yo, k2tog, yo, k2, repeat *...* until 14 sts before end, k1, yo, ssk, yo, sk2p, yo, k2tog, yo, k3, yo, k3

Row 17: (sl1, k2), yo, k5, yo, ssk, k1, k2tog, yo, k3, *k2, yo, ssk, k1, k2tog, yo, k3*, repeat *...* until 12 sts before **CS**, k2, yo, ssk, k1, k2tog, yo, k5, yo, k1 (**CS**), yo, k5, yo, ssk, k1, k2tog, yo, k3, repeat *...* until 15 sts before end, k2, yo, ssk, k1, k2tog, yo, k5, yo, k3

Row 19: (sl1, k2), yo, k1, k2tog, yo, k1, yo, ssk, k1, yo, sk2p, yo, k1, k2tog, yo, k1, *yo, ssk, k1, yo, sk2p, yo, k1, k2tog, yo, k1*, repeat *...* until 13 sts before **CS**, yo, ssk, k1, yo, sk2p, yo, k1, k2tog, yo, k1, yo, ssk, k1, yo, k1 (**CS**), yo, k1, k2tog, yo, k1, yo, ssk, k1, yo, sk2p, yo, k1, k2tog, yo, k1, repeat *...* until 16 sts before end, yo, ssk, k1, yo, sk2p, yo, k1, k2tog, yo, k1, yo, ssk, k1, yo, k3

Ending Row 20 of the **Main Ripple Lace** with *85 sts total*.
(39 sts between CS and garter stitch edges on each side).

Continue with the **Transition Rows** on the following page.

4. Transition Rows between Main Ripple Lace and **Modified Fan Shell Lace**:

Row 1 *(rs)*: (sl1, k2), yo, k to **CS,** yo, k1, yo, knit to last 3 sts, yo, k3
Row 2 *(ws)*: (sl1, k2), purl to **CS**, k1tbl, purl to last 3 sts, k3
Row 3: repeat Row 1

Ending Row 3 of this transition section with *93 sts total.*
(43 sts between CS and garter edges on each side).
Continue with the **Modified Fan Shell Lace Pattern I** below.

5. Modified Fan Shell Pattern I:

Row 1 *(ws)*: (sl1, k2), *p7, (k11, p7)2x*, k1tbl, repeat *...*, k3
Row 2 *(rs)*: (sl1, k2), yo, *k7, (p11, k7)2x*, yo, k1 (**CS**), yo, repeat *...*, yo, k3
Row 3: (sl1, k2), *p6, p2tog, p11, p2tbl, p3, p2tog, k11, p2tbl, p6*, k1tbl, repeat *...*, k3
Row 4: (sl1, k2), yo, k6, *ssk, k9, k2tog*, k3, repeat *...*, k6, yo, k1 (**CS**), yo, k6, repeat *...*, k3, repeat *...*, k6, yo, k3
Row 5: (sl1, k2), *p7, p2tog, p7, p2tbl, p3, p2tog, p7, p2tbl, p7*, k1tbl, repeat *...*, k3
Row 6: (sl1, k2), yo, *k9, (yo, k1)5x, yo, k7, (yo, k1)5x, yo, k9*, yo, k1 (**CS**), yo, repeat *...*, yo, k3
Row 7: (sl1, k2), *p10, k11, p7, k11, p10*, k1tbl, repeat *...*, k3
Row 8: (sl1, k2), yo, *k10, p11, k7, p11, k10*, yo, k1 (**CS**), yo, repeat *...*, yo, k3
Row 9: (sl1, k2), *p9, p2tog, p11, p2tbl, p3, p2tog, p11, p2tbl, p9*, k1tbl, repeat *...*, k3
Row 10: (sl1, k2), yo, *k9, ssk, k9, k2tog, k3, ssk, k9, k2tog, k9*, yo, k1 (**CS**), yo, repeat *...*, yo, k3
Row 11: (sl1, k2), *p10, p2tog, p7, p2tbl, p3, p2tog, p7, p2tbl, p10*, k1tbl, repeat *...*, k3

Row 13: (sl1, k2), *p13, k11, p7, k11, p13*, k1tbl, repeat *...*, k3

Ending Row 13 of the **Modified Fan Shell Pattern I** with *117 sts total.*
(55 sts between CS and garter edges on each side).
Continue with the Transition Rows below.

6. Transition Rows between Modified Fan Shell Lace I and **Main Ripple Lace**:

Row 1 *(rs)*: (sl1, k2), yo, k to **CS**, yo, k1, yo, knit to last 3 sts, yo, k3
Row 2 *(ws)*: (sl1, k2), purl to **CS**, k1tbl, purl to last 3 sts, k3
Row 3: (sl1, k2), yo, k27, sk2p, k27 to **CS**; yo, k1, yo, k27, sk2p, k27, yo, k3
Row 4: (sl1, k2), p2, m1p, p to 2 sts before **CS**, m1p, p2, k1tbl, p2, m1p, purl to 5 sts before end, m1p, p2, k3

Ending Row 4 of this transition section with *123 sts total.*
(58 sts between CS and garter edges on each side).

Continue with the **Main Ripple Lace** pattern.

Complete the **Main Ripple Lace** pattern a total of **2** times - *40 rows in all.*

Ending Row 40 of the **Main Ripple Lace** pattern with *205 sts total.*
(99 sts between CS and garter edges on each side).
Continue with the Transition Rows below.

7. Transition Rows between Main Ripple Lace and **Modified Fan Shell Lace II**:

Row 1 *(rs)*: (sl1, k2), yo, (k33, m1)3x to **CS**, yo, k1 (**CS**), yo,

Row 2 *(ws)***:** (sl1, k2), purl to **CS**, k1tbl, purl to last 3 sts, k3
Row 3: (sl1, k2), yo, (k34, m1)3x, k2 to **CS**, yo, k1 (**CS**), yo, k2, (m1, k34)3x to last 3 sts, yo, k3

Ending Row 4 of this transition section with ***225 sts total.***
(109 sts between CS and garter edges on each side).

Continue with the **Modified Fan Shell Lace Pattern II**
below.

8. Modified Fan Shell Lace Pattern II:

Row 1 *(ws)***:** (sl1, k2), p4, *k11, p4*, repeat from *...* to **CS**, k1tbl, p4, repeat *...* to the last 3 sts, k3
Row 2 *(rs)***:** (sl1, k2), yo, k4, *p11, k4*, repeat from *...* to **CS**, yo, k1 (**CS**), yo, k4, repeat *...* to the last 3 sts, yo, k3
Row 3: (sl1, k2), p3, *p2tog, p11, p2tbl*, repeat from *...* until 3 sts before **CS**, p3, k1tbl, repeat from *...* to last 6 sts, p3, k3
Row 4: (sl1, k2), yo, k3, *ssk, k9, k2tog*, repeat from *...* until 3 sts before **CS**, k3, yo, k1 (**CS**), yo, k3, repeat *...* to last 6 sts, k3, yo, k3
Row 5: (sl1, k2), p4, *p2tog, p7, p2tbl*, repeat from *...* to 4 sts before **CS**, p4, k1tbl, p4, repeat *...* to 7 sts before end, p4, k3
Row 6: (sl1, k2), yo, k6, *(yo, k1)5x, yo, k4*, repeat *...*, *(ending with a k6 instead of a k4)* to **CS**, yo, k1 (**CS**), yo, k6, repeat *...* *(ending with a k6 instead of a k4)* to last 3 sts, yo, k3
Row 7: (sl1, k2), p7, *k11, p4*, repeat *...* *(ending with a p7 instead of p4)* to **CS**, ktbl, p7, repeat *...* *(ending with a k7 instead of k4)* to last 3 sts, k3
Row 8: (sl1, k2), yo, k7, *p11, k4*, repeat *...* *(ending with a k7 instead of k4)* to **CS**, yo, k1 (**CS**), yo, k7, repeat *...* *(ending with a k7 instead of k4)* to last 3 sts, yo, k3
Row 9: (sl1, k2), p6, *p2tog, k11, p2tbl*, repeat *...* until 6 sts before **CS**, p6, k1tbl, p6, repeat *...* to last 9 sts, p6, k3

Row 10: (sl1, k2), yo, k6, *ssk, k9, k2tog*, repeat *...* until 6 sts before **CS**, k6, yo, k1 (**CS**), yo, k6, repeat *...* to last 9 sts, k6, yo, k3

Row 11: (sl1, k2), p7, *p2tog, p7, p2tbl*, repeat *...* until 7 sts before **CS**, p7, k1tbl, p7, repeat *...* to last 10 sts, p7, k3

Row 12: (sl1, k2), yo, k9, *(yo, k1)5x, yo, k4*, repeat *...* *(ending with a k9 instead of a k4)* to **CS**, yo, k1 (**CS**), yo, k9, repeat *...* *(ending with a k9 instead of k4)* to last 3 sts, yo, k3

Row 13: (sl1, k2), p10, *k11, p4*, repeat *...* *(ending with a p10 instead of p4)* to **CS**, k1tbl, p10, repeat *...* *(ending with a p10 instead of p4)* to last 3 sts, k3

Ending Row 13 of this **Modified Fan Shell Lace II** section with *249 sts total*. *(121 sts between CS and garter edges on each side).* Continue with the Transition Rows below.

9. Transition Rows between Fan Shell Lace II and **Main Ripple Lace** pattern:

Row 1 *(rs):* (sl1, k2), yo, ssk, k6, k2tog, k to 10 sts before the **CS**, ssk, k6, k2tog, yo, k1 (**CS**), yo, ssk, k6, k2tog, k to 13 sts before end, ssk, k6, k2tog, yo, k3

Row 2 *(ws):* (sl1, k2), purl to **CS**, k1tbl, p to last 3 sts, k3

Row 3: (sl1, k2), yo, k to 8 sts before the **CS**, ssk, k4, k2tog, yo, k1 (**CS**), yo, ssk, k4, k2tog, k to 3 sts before end, yo, k3

Row 4: (sl1, k2), purl to **CS**, k1tbl, p to last 3 sts, k3

Ending Row 4 of this transition section with *245 sts total*. *(119 sts between CS and garter edges on each side)*

Continue with **2 full repeats** of the **Main Ripple Lace** pattern as completed previously- *40 rows total.*

Ending Row 40 of this **Main Ripple Lace** section *(second repeat)* with *325 sts total.* *(159 sts between CS and garter edges on each side)*

Continue with the Transition Rows below.

10. Transition Rows between Main Ripple Lace pattern and **Queen's Goblet** pattern:

Row 1 *(rs):* (sl1, k2), yo, knit to **CS**, yo, k1 (**CS**), yo, knit to last 3 sts, yo, k3

Row 2 *(ws):* (sl1, k2), p to **CS**, k1tbl, p to 3 sts before end, k3

Row 3: repeat Row 1

Row 4: (sl1, k2), k across to **CS**, k1tbl, k to last 3 sts, k3

Ending Row 4 of this transition section with *333 sts total.* *(163 sts between CS and garter edges on each side).*

Continue with the **Queen's Goblet** *or* **Queen's Mirror** pattern below.

11a. Queen's Goblet Pattern: *(There will be 2 sts between each goblet.)*

NOTE- *add stitch markers as you start knitting row 5. Stitch marker placement will be denoted by (PM) and slip marker by (SM). This will help you keep track of where the goblets are in the pattern.*

Row 1 (rs): (sl1, k2), yo, k to **CS**, yo, k1 (**CS**), yo, k to last 3 sts, yo, k3

Row 2 (ws): (sl1, k2), m1L, p to **CS**, k1tbl (**CS**), p to last 3 sts, m1R, k3

Row 3: repeat row 1

Row 4: repeat row 2

Row 5: (sl1, k2), PM, yo, k1, PM, *[(k1, p17, k1), k2, PM]7x, [(k1, p17, k1), k1, PM]* to **CS**, yo, PM, k1 (**CS**), PM, yo, k1, PM, repeat *...* to last 3 sts, yo, PM, k3

Row 6 and all following ws rows to Row 32: (sl1, k2), SM, p to next m, SM, *k all k sts and p all p sts* to 2 st markers before **CS**, SM, p to next m, SM, k1tbl (**CS**), SM, p to next m,

27

SM, repeat *...* to last 2 st markers, SM, purl to last st marker, SM, k3

Row 7: (sl1, k2), SM, yo, k to next m, SM, *[(k1, p17, k1), k2, SM]7x, [(k1, p17, k1), k1, SM]*, k to next m, yo, SM, k1 (**CS**), SM, yo, k to next m, SM, repeat *...*, k to next m, yo, SM, k3

Row 9: (sl1, k2), SM, yo, k to next m, SM, *[(p19), k2, SM]7x, [(p19), k1, SM]*, k to next m, yo, SM, k1 (**CS**), SM, yo, k to next m, SM, repeat *...*, k to next m, yo, SM, k3

Row 11: repeat row 9

Row 13: (sl1, k2), SM, yo, k to next m, SM, *[(k3, p13, k3), k2, SM]7x, [(k3, p13, k3), k1, SM]*, k to next m, yo, SM, k1 (**CS**), SM, yo, k to next m, SM, repeat *...*, k to next m, yo, SM, k3

Row 15: (sl1, k2), SM, yo, k to next m, SM, *[(k4, p11, k4), k2, SM]7x, [(k4, p11, k4), k1, SM]*, k to next m, yo, SM, k1 (**CS**), SM, yo, k to next m, SM, repeat *...*, k to next m, yo, SM, k3

Row 17: (sl1, k2), SM, yo, k to next m, SM, *[(k6, p7, k6), k2, SM]7x, [(k6, p7, k6), k1, SM]*, k to next m, yo, SM, k1 (**CS**), SM, yo, k to next m, SM, repeat *...*, k to next m, yo, SM, k3

Row 19: repeat row 17

Row 21: (sl1, k2), SM, yo, k to next m, SM, *[(k8, p3, k8), k2, SM]7x, [(k8, p3, k8), k1, SM]*, k to next m, yo, SM, k1 (**CS**), SM, yo, k to next m, SM, repeat *...*, k to next m, yo, SM, k3

Row 23: repeat row 21

Row 25: repeat row 21

Row 27: repeat row 21

Row 29: repeat row 17

Row 31: repeat row 15

Row 33: repeat row 1 *(removing st markers as you go)*

Row 34: (sl1, k2), purl to **CS**, k1tbl (**CS**), purl to last 3 sts, k3

Row 35: repeat row 1

Row 36: (sl1, k2), purl to **CS**, k1tbl (**CS**), purl to last 3 sts, k3

Ending Row 36 of this **Queen's Goblet** section with ***405 sts total.***
(199 sts between CS and garter edges on each side).
Continue with the **Transition Rows** after the mirror section.

11b. Queen's Mirror Pattern:
(There will be 2 sts between each mirror.)

NOTE - add stitch markers as you start knitting row 5. Stitch marker placement will be denoted by *(PM)* and slip marker by *(SM)*. This will help you keep track of where the goblets are in the pattern.

Row 1 (rs): (sl1, k2), yo, knit to **CS**, yo, k1 (**CS**), yo, knit to last 3 sts, yo, k3

Row 2 (ws): (sl1, k2), m1L, p to **CS**, k1tbl (**CS**), p to last 3 sts, m1R, k3

Row 3: repeat row 1

Row 4: repeat row 2

Row 5: (sl1, k2), PM, yo, k1, PM, *[(p19), k2, PM]7x, [(p19), k1, PM]* to **CS**, yo, PM, k1 (**CS**), PM, yo, k1, PM, repeat *...* to last 3 sts, yo, PM, k3

Row 6: (sl1, k2), SM, p to next m, SM, *[p1, (k19)], SM, [p2, (k19), SM]7x* to 2 st markers before **CS**, SM, p to next m, SM, k1tbl (**CS**), SM, p to next m, SM, repeat *...* to last 2 st markers, SM, purl to last st marker, SM, k3

Row 7: (sl1, k2), SM, yo, k to next m, SM, *[(p2, p15, p2), k2, SM]7x, [(p2, p15, p2), k1, SM]*, k to next m, yo, SM, k1 (**CS**), SM, yo, k to next m, SM, repeat *...*, k to next m, yo, SM, k3

Row 8: (sl1, k2), SM, p to next m, SM, * [p1, (k2, p15, k2)], SM, [p2, (k2, p15, k2), SM]7x* to 2 st markers before **CS**, SM, p to next m, SM, k1tbl (**CS**), SM, p to next m, SM, repeat *...* to last 2 st markers, SM, purl to last st marker, SM, k3

Row 9: (sl1, k2), SM, yo, k to next m, SM, *[(p2, k6, p3, k6, p2), k2, SM]7x, [(p2, k6, p3, k6, p2), k1, SM]*, k to next m, yo, SM, k1 (**CS**), SM, yo, k to next m, SM, repeat *...*, k to next m, yo, SM, k3

Row 10: (sl1, k2), SM, p to next m, SM, * [p1, (k2, p4, k7, p4, k2)], SM, [p2, (k2, p4, k7, p4, k2), SM]7x* to 2 st markers before **CS**, SM, p to next m, SM, k1tbl (**CS**), SM, p to next m, SM, repeat *...* to last 2 st markers, SM, purl to last st marker, SM, k3

28

Row 11: (sl1, k2), SM, yo, k to next m, SM, *[(p2, k3, p9, k3, p2), k2, SM]7x, [(p2, k3, p9, k3, p2), k1, SM]*, k to next m, yo, SM, k1 (CS), SM, yo, k to next m, SM, repeat *...*, k to next m, yo, SM, k3

Row 12: (sl1, k2), SM, p to next m, SM, * [p1, (k2, p2, k3, p5, k3, p2, k2)], SM, [p2, (k2, p2, k3, p5, k3, p2, k2), SM]7x to 2 st markers before CS, SM, p to next m, SM, k1tbl (CS), SM, p to next m, SM, repeat *...* to last 2 st markers, SM, purl to last st marker, SM, k3

Row 13: (sl1, k2), SM, yo, k to next m, SM, *[(p2, k2, p3, k9, p3, k2, p2), k2, SM]7x, [(p2, k2, p3, k9, p3, k2, p2), k1, SM]*, k to next m, yo, SM, k1 (CS), SM, yo, k to next m, SM, repeat *...*, k to next m, yo, SM, k3

Row 14: (sl1, k2), SM, p to next m, SM, * [p1, (k2, p1, k3, p7, k3, p1, k2)], SM, [p2, (k2, p1, k3, p7, k3, p1, k2), SM]7x* to 2 st markers before CS, SM, p to next m, SM, k1tbl (CS), SM, p to next m, SM, repeat *...* to last 2 st markers, SM, purl to last st marker, SM, k3

Row 15: (sl1, k2), SM, yo, k to next m, SM, *[(p2, k1, p3, k7, p3, k1, p2), k2, SM]7x, [(p2, k1, p3, k7, p3, k1, p2), k1, SM]*, k to next m, yo, SM, k1 (CS), SM, yo, k to next m, SM, repeat *...*, k to next m, yo, SM, k3

Row 16: repeat Row 14

Row 17: repeat Row 15

Row 18: repeat Row 14

Row 19: repeat Row 15

Row 20: repeat Row 14

Row 21: (sl1, k2), SM, yo, k to next m, SM, *[(p2, k1, p4, k6, p2, k2, p2), k2, SM]7x, [(p2, k1, p4, k6, p2, k2, p2), k1, SM]*, k to next m, yo, SM, k1 (CS), SM, yo, k to next m, SM, repeat *...*, k to next m, yo, SM, k3

Row 22: (sl1, k2), SM, p to next m, SM, * [p1, (k2, p2, k3, p5, k3, p2, k2)], SM, [p2, (k2, p2, k3, p5, k3, p2, k2), SM]7x* to 2 st markers before CS, SM, p to next m, SM, k1tbl (CS), SM, p to next m, SM, repeat *...* to last 2 st markers, SM, purl to last st marker, SM, k3

Row 23: (sl1, k2), SM, yo, k to next m, SM, *[(p2, k2, p4, k3, p3, k3, p2), k2, SM]7x, [(p2, k2, p4, k3, p3, k3, p2), k1, SM]*, k to next m, yo, SM, k1 (CS), SM, yo, k to next m, SM, repeat *...*, k to next m, yo, SM, k3

Row 24: (sl1, k2), SM, p to next m, SM, * [p1, (k2, p4, k8, p3, k2)], SM, [p2, (k2, p4, k8, p3, k2), SM]7x* to 2 st markers before CS, SM, p to next m, SM, k1tbl (CS), SM, p to next m, SM, repeat *...* to last 2 st markers, SM, purl to last st marker, SM, k3

Row 25: (sl1, k2), SM, yo, k to next m, SM, *[(p2, k4, p7, k4, p2), k2, SM]7x, [(p2, k4, p7, k4, p2), k1, SM]*, k to next m, yo, SM, k1 (CS), SM, yo, k to next m, SM, repeat *...*, k to next m, yo, SM, k3

Row 26: (sl1, k2), SM, p to next m, SM, * [p1, (k2, p1, k7, p7, k2)], SM, [p2, (k2, p1, k7, p7, k2), SM]7x* to 2 st markers before CS, SM, p to next m, SM, k1tbl (CS), SM, p to next m, SM, repeat *...* to last 2 st markers, SM, purl to last st marker, SM, k3

Row 27: (sl1, k2), SM, yo, k to next m, SM, *[(p2, k9, p5, k1, p2), k2, SM]7x, [(p2, k9, p5, k1, p2), k1, SM]*, k to next m, yo, SM, k1 (CS), SM, yo, k to next m, SM, repeat *...*, k to next m, yo, SM, k3

Row 28: (sl1, k2), SM, p to next m, SM, * [p1, (k2, p1, k2, p12, k2)], SM, [p2, (k2, p1, k2, p12, k2), SM]7x* to 2 st markers before CS, SM, p to next m, SM, k1tbl (CS), SM, p to next m, SM, repeat *...* to last 2 st markers, SM, purl to last st marker, SM, k3

Row 29: (sl1, k2), SM, yo, k to next m, SM, *[(p2, p15, p2), k2, SM]7x, [(p2, p15, p2), k1, SM]*, k to next m, yo, SM, k1 (CS), SM, yo, k to next m, SM, repeat *...*, k to next m, yo, SM, k3

Row 30: (sl1, k2), SM, p to next m, SM, * [p1, (k2, p15, k2)], SM, [p2, (k2, p15, k2), SM]7x* to 2 st markers before CS, SM, p to next m, SM, k1tbl (CS), SM, p to next m, SM, repeat *...* to last 2 st markers, SM, purl to last st marker, SM, k3

Row 31: (sl1, k2), SM, yo, k1, SM, *[(p19), k2, SM]7x, [(p19), k1, SM]* to **CS**, yo, SM, k1 (**CS**), SM, yo, k1, SM, repeat *...*

to last 3 sts, yo, SM, k

Row 32: (sl1, k2), SM, p to next m, SM, *[p1, (k19)], SM, [p2, (k19), SM]7x* to 2 st markers before **CS**, SM, p to next m, SM, k1tbl (**CS**), SM, p to next m, SM, repeat *...* to last 2 st markers, SM, purl to last st marker, SM, k3

Row 33: repeat row 1 *(removing st markers as you go)*

Row 34: (sl1, k2), purl to **CS**, k1tbl (**CS**), purl to last 3 sts, k3

Row 35: repeat row 1

Row 36: (sl1, k2), purl to **CS**, k1tbl (**CS**), purl to last 3 sts, k3

Ending Row 36 of this **Queen's Mirror** section with ***405 sts total***.
(199 sts between CS and garter edges on each side).

Continue with the Transition Rows below.

12. Transition Rows between Queen's Goblet/Mirror pattern and **Modified Daisy Chain Lace** edging:

Row 1 *(rs)***:** (sl1, k2), yo, p to CS, yo, k1 (**CS**), yo, p to 3 sts before end, yo, k3

Row 2 *(ws)***:** (sl1, k2), k to CS, k1tbl (**CS**), k to last 3 sts, k3

Row 3: (sl1, k2),*yo, k2tog*; repeat *...* to 1 st before CS, k1, yo, k1 (**CS**), yo, k1, repeat *...* to last 3 sts, , yo, k3

Row 4: sl1, knit to end

Row 5 *(rs)***:** (sl1, k2), purl to last 3 sts, k3

Ending Row 5 of this transition section with ***413 sts total***.
(203 sts between CS and garter edges on each side).

Switching to the laceweight yarn, begin the **Modified Daisy Chain Lace** pattern:

13. Modified Daisy Chain Lace: *(multiple of 6 sts +1)*

Row 1 *(ws)***:** (sl1, k2), m1L, knit to 3 sts before end, m1R, k3

Row 2 *(rs)***:** (sl1, k2), k1,*(k1 by wrapping yarn 3x around the needle instead of 1x)5x, k1*; repeat from *...* to last 3 sts, k3
*(**68 repeat**s of the Daisy Chain Lace pattern)*

Row 3: (sl1, k2), k1,*(work **cluster stitch** over 5 sts), k1*; repeat from *...* to last 3 sts, k3

Row 4: (sl1, k2), knit to end

Row 5: (sl1, k2), knit to end

Row 6: (sl1, k2), knit to end

Row 7: *(*sl1, k2), k4, *(k1 by wrapping yarn 3x around the needle instead of 1x)5x, k1*; repeat from *...* to 6 sts before end, k6 *(**67 repeat**s of the Daisy Chain Lace pattern)*

Row 8: *(*sl1, k2), k4, *(work **cluster stitch** over 5 sts), k1*; repeat from *...* to 6 sts before end, k6

Row 9: (sl1, k2), knit to end

Row 10: (sl1, k2), knit to end

Cluster stitch: With yarn in front, (sl next stitch, dropping extra yarn overs)5x, (bring yarn around to the back, sl 5 sts back to the left hand needle, bring the yarn back to the front, sl 5 sts to the right hand needle)2x.

Using the **larger needle size**, bind off your stitches loosely **on the wrong side** with this **K2TBL Bind Off** technique:

Knit the first stitch, *knit a st, place the stitches from the right hand needle to the left hand needle, knit the next two stitches together through the back loop*. *Repeat from *...* for each stitch until all stitches are bound off.* Weave in all ends.

14. Finishing:

Fill a basin with tepid water. Add a capful of no rinse wool wash, like Eucalan or Soak. Add a capful of scented hair conditioner *(if desired)*. Place your finished shawl into the basin and let soak overnight or at least 3 hours. Gently squeeze out all excess water from your shawl without wringing it.

Place the shawl in a lingerie/net washing bag and place on the *spin-only* cycle in your washing machine. Lay your shawl out flat on a surface that won't be disturbed for at least 12-24 hours. *(I like to use my bed or bedroom floor with foam puzzle blocking boards).* Beginning at the top center of your shawl, use t-pins or blocking wires to stretch out your shawl to the desired measurements along the top straight edge. *(Try not to pull too much on the damp, fragile fabric, but enough so that you can see the lace pattern "open up".)* Pin the center bottom next and then work out to each side, making sure that each side looks even. Let your shawl remain pinned until completely dry.

Queen's Goblet

Row	19	18	17	16	15	14	13	12	11	10	9	8	7	6	5	4	3	2	1	Row
32						•	•	•	•	•	•	•	•	•						
						•	•	•	•	•	•	•	•							31
30							•	•	•	•	•	•								
							•	•	•	•	•	•								29
28									•	•	•									
									•	•	•									27
26									•	•	•									
									•	•	•									25
24									•	•	•									
									•	•	•									23
22									•	•	•									
									•	•	•									21
20							•	•	•	•	•	•	•							
							•	•	•	•	•	•								19
18							•	•	•	•	•	•								
							•	•	•	•	•	•								17
16					•	•	•	•	•		•	•	•	•						
					•	•	•	•	•	•	•	•	•							15
14				•	•	•	•	•	•	•	•	•	•		•					
				•	•	•	•	•	•	•	•	•	•		•					13
12	•	•	•	•	•			•	•	•	•	•	•	•	•		•	•	•	
	•	•	•	•	•			•	•	•	•	•	•	•	•		•	•	•	11
10	•	•	•	•			•	•	•	•	•	•	•	•	•		•	•	•	
	•	•	•	•			•	•	•	•	•	•	•	•	•		•	•		9
8		•	•	•	•	•	•	•	•	•	•	•	•	•	•	•	•			
		•	•	•	•	•	•	•	•	•	•	•	•	•	•	•	•			7
6		•	•	•	•	•	•	•	•	•	•	•	•	•	•	•	•			
		•	•	•	•	•	•	•	•	•	•	•	•	•	•	•	•			5

31

Key

☐	Knit k (RS) Knit (WS) Purl	↗	Purl 2 Together Tbl p2tog tbl (RS) Purl 2 stitches together through back loop
⅄	K1 tbl k1 tbl (RS) knit 1 stitch through back loop	✗	Sl2 Kwise K1 Psso s2kp (RS) slip 2 sts knitwise, k1, pass the slipped sts over
╱	Knit 2 Together k2tog (RS) Knit 2 stitches together	⅀	SK2P sk2p (RS) Slip K2tog PSSO
⅄	Knit 3 Together k3tog (RS) Knit 3 stitches together	△	Slip Knit Pass Over skp (RS) Slip 1, knit 1, pass slipped stitch over
⅄	Knit 3 Together Tbl k3tog tbl (RS) knit 3 stitches together through back loop	⅄	Slip With Yarn In Back slip wyib (RS) yarn in back (WS) Slip stitch as if to purl, holding yarn in the front
M	Make One Knitwise m1 (RS) Make one by lifting strand in between stitch just worked and the next stitch, knit into back of this thread	╲	Slip Slip Knit ssk (RS) slip, slip, knit slipped sts together
M	Make One Purlwise m1p (RS) Make one by lifting strand in between stitch just worked and the next stitch, purl into back of this thread	■	No Stitch x (RS) No Stitch (WS) No Stitch
•	Purl p (RS) Purl (WS) Knit	O	Yarn Over yo (RS) Yarn Over
╱	Purl 2 Together p2tog (RS) Purl 2 Together		

Beginning Ripple Lace

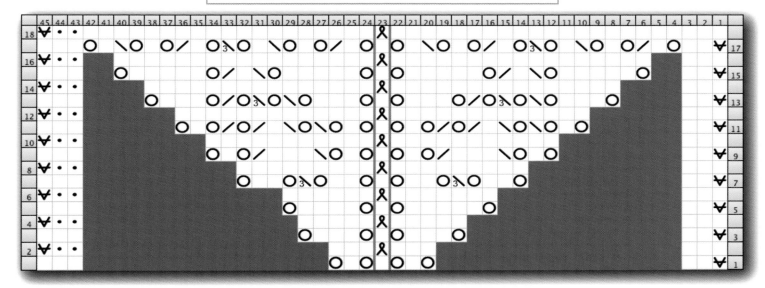

RED indicates st markers on each side of the center stitch (**CS**).

CHARTS NOTE:

You may have noticed that there are <u>a number of charts missing</u> for this pattern. I tried *(a number of times)* to create these charts, but they got so large *(widthwise and by sheer number of them)*, that I was unable to arrange them in the book with any satisfaction. I know that there are a lot of directions to read to knit this lace pattern and charts would help. I'm going to do my best to create some more charts that will be available as a **free download** on my website. Until then, feel free to create your own, using the key that I have used or follow the written instructions only. I apologize for this inconvenience.

SHAWLETTE OPTION:

My friend, **Sarah**, recommended a lovely option for this shawl. If you'd like to knit a smaller shawl *(or shawlette)*, you could leave out the picture *(Queen's Goblet/Mirror)* part entirely. You could end with the **Transition Rows** between the **Main Ripple Lace** and **Queen's Goblet** pattern and then follow the **Modified Daisy Chain** lace pattern after making this change:

13. Modified Daisy Chain Lace: *(multiple of 6 sts +1)*

Row 1 *(ws):* (sl1, k2), k2tog, knit to 5 sts before end, ssk, k3 *(331 sts) and (54 repeats of the **Modified Daisy Chain Lace** pattern).*

Follow the rest of the instructions as shown.

Water Nymph Washcloths

Hans Christian Andersen's "*Little Mermaid*" fairytale influenced this quick-to-knit pattern. The washcloths have an attractive, mermaid-tail pattern that is wonderfully smooth in texture. The cotton yarn is very nice to knit with and has a wonderful drape. The more you use these washcloths, the softer they become. They would be a delightful addition to any bathroom or kitchen.

34

Pattern Difficulty:

Yarn:
(1) 3 oz/85 g skein (153 yds/140 m) of **Hobby Lobby's** *I Love This Cotton* (100% cotton) in "aqua ombre #64".

NOTE: One large washcloth uses approximately **97 yards**/88.7 m of yarn and the small washcloth uses **52 yards**/47.6 cm of yarn. You can knit **BOTH** one large and one small washcloth from 1 skein of this yarn.

Needle: US **7** (4.5 mm) in either a 24"/61 cm circular (or a set of straights) or needle size necessary to obtain gauge

Gauge: 5 sts and **6** rows = 1"/2.5 cm (stockinette)

Notions: 4-6 stitch markers, scissors, tapestry needle, row counter, measuring tape

Finished Size:
(large) **11" x 11"**/28 cm x 28 cm *(unblocked)*
(small) **9" x 8.5"**/22.8 cm x 21.6 cm *(unblocked)*

*In the suggested gauge, each repeat of the **Chevron Lace** pattern measures **3.5"**/8.9 cm wide and **1.25"**/3.2 cm tall, if you'd like to vary the size of the washcloth.*

Directions

A. LARGE WASHCLOTH:

CO **50 sts**, loosely.

*(If you'd like a neater edge, **slip the first stitch** of every row.)*

Knit **3** rows.
On the 4th row, **place stitch markers** onto the work: k3, pm, k16, pm, k3, pm, k6, pm, k3, pm, k16, pm, k3. *(Stitch markers are optional if you feel comfortable following the lace pattern without them. Slip markers as you follow the pattern.)*

1. Body of Washcloth:

Row 1: k3, follow **Chevron Lace** pattern, k12, follow **Chevron Lace** pattern, k3
Row 2: k3, **Chevron Lace** pattern, k3, p6, k3, **Chevron Lace** pattern, k3

Repeat Rows 1 and 2 until washcloth measures **10.5"**/26.7 cm, or **8 repeats** of the **Chevron Lace** pattern.

Next row: k3, purl to 3 sts before end, k3
Repeat the row above 2 more times - **3 rows total**.
BO loosely *(in pattern)* on the next row.

B. SMALL WASHCLOTH:

CO **38 sts** loosely.

*(If you'd like a neater edge, **slip the first stitch** of every row.)*

Knit **1** row.

On the 2nd row, **place stitch markers** onto the work: k2, pm, k16, pm, k2, pm, k16, pm, k2.
(Stitch markers are optional if you feel comfortable following the lace pattern without them.)

1. Body of Washcloth:

Row 1: k2, follow **Chevron Lace** pattern, k2, follow **Chevron Lace** pattern, k2
Row 2: k2, **Chevron Lace** pattern*, k2, **Chevron Lace** pattern*, k2
(the Chevron Lace pattern on this row will be purl all sts)

Repeat Rows 1 and 2 until washcloth measures **8"/**20.3 cm, or **6 repeats** of the **Chevron Lace** pattern.

Next row: k2, purl to 2 sts before end, k2
Repeat the row above one more time - **2 rows total.**

BO loosely *(in pattern)* on the next row.

2. Finishing:

Weave in all ends neatly. You may wish to lightly steam the washcloths *(under a press cloth and with the right side down)* to open up the lace a bit or give them a soak/wash and spin in the dryer.

Key

☐ Knit k (RS) Knit (WS) Purl	⊠ Purl 2 Together Tbl p2tog tbl (RS) Purl 2 stitches together through back loop
🎗 K1 tbl k1 tbl (RS) knit 1 stitch through back loop	✖ Sl2 Kwise K1 Psso s2kp (RS) slip 2 sts knitwise, k1, pass the slipped sts over
✓ Knit 2 Together k2tog (RS) Knit 2 stitches together	⅗ SK2P sk2p (RS) Slip K2tog PSSO
⬔ Knit 3 Together k3tog (RS) Knit 3 stitches together	△ Slip Knit Pass Over skp (RS) Slip 1, knit 1, pass slipped stitch over
⬕ Knit 3 Together Tbl k3tog tbl (RS) knit 3 stitches together through back loop	☡ Slip With Yarn In Back slip wyib (RS) yarn in back (WS) Slip stitch as if to purl, holding yarn in the front
Ⓜ Make One Knitwise m1 (RS) Make one by lifting strand in between stitch just worked and the next stitch, knit into back of this thread	⟍ Slip Slip Knit ssk (RS) slip, slip, knit slipped sts together
Ⓜ Make One Purlwise m1p (RS) Make one by lifting strand in between stitch just worked and the next stitch, purl into back of this thread	▪ No Stitch x (RS) No Stitch (WS) No Stitch
▪ Purl p (RS) Purl (WS) Knit	Ⓞ Yarn Over yo (RS) Yarn Over
✓• Purl 2 Together p2tog (RS) Purl 2 Together	

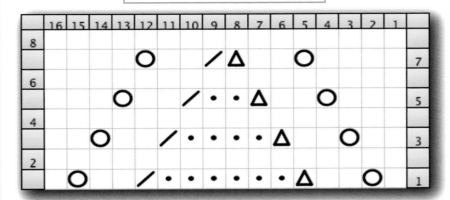

Chevron Lace

Chevron Lace: *(16 stitch repeat)*

Row 1 *(rs)*: k1, yo, k2, skp, p6, k2tog, k2, yo, k1
Row 2 *(ws)* **and all even rows:** purl
Row 3: k2, yo, k2, skp, p4, k2tog, k2, yo, k2
Row 5: k3, yo, k2, skp, p2, k2tog, k2, yo, k3
Row 7: k4, yo, k2, skp, k2tog, k2, yo, k4
Row 8: purl

Repeat Rows 1-8 for pattern.

37

Violet's Garden Socks

This enchanting and feminine sock design features a flowery lace pattern along the top of the foot and side of the leg.   The pattern represents the Talking Flowers (especially the shy Violet) in Lewis Carroll's "**Through the Looking Glass**".   The yarn is soft and warm, while the slight color variation shows off the lace pattern beautifully.   These socks are cozy and comfortable as well as ideal for wearing with either fancy clogs or sneakers. The lace and ribbing patterns on the leg and foot are very flexible, creating a more versatile and personalized fit.

Pattern Difficulty:

Yarn:

(1) 4 oz/113.4 g skein (380 yds/347.5 m) of **Three Irish Girls'** *Finley Fingering* (100% merino wool) in "larkspur" OR (**308**){**380**} yds/(281.6){347.5} m or 4 oz/113.4 g of a heavy fingering weight merino wool yarn.

Needle: **US 2** (2.75 mm) in either a 32-40"/81-102 cm circular for Magic Loop, (2) 24"/61 cm circulars *(denoted by* **N1, N2**) or a set of 5 dpns *(denoted by n1, n2, n3, n4)* or needle size necessary to obtain gauge

Gauge: **7** sts and **9** rows = 1"/2.5 cm (stockinette)

Notions: clip-on stitch marker *(or safety pin)*, small stitch markers, row counter, scissors, tapestry needle, measuring tape, sock blockers *(optional)*.

Finished Size:
(women's medium)
8.5"/21.6 cm ankle, **10-11"**/25.4-27.9 cm leg, 9.5"/24.1 cm foot*
{*women's large*}
9.5"/24.1 cm ankle, **12-13"**/30.5-33 cm leg, 10.5"/26.7 cm foot*

*Length of foot can be adjusted easily by adding (or subtracting) rounds to the foot section before starting toe decreases. Extra yarn may be needed for a longer foot.

Directions (**RIGHT** sock)

1. Cuff:

CO (**66**) {**70**} sts. Being careful that the sts aren't twisted, join in the round. Clip a stitch marker to the very first stitch to denote the beginning of the round. As you continue to knit the sock, you should occasionally move the clipped st marker up to the appropriate stitch above.

Distribute your stitches evenly over your **2** *(or 4)* needles. Half the stitches on **N1** *(n1/n2)* and the other half on **N2** *(n3/n4)*.

(Medium size)
First round: (**Baby Shale Stitch** over the next 11 sts, PM)6x across round.
Next round: (follow the next round of the **Baby Shale Stitch** over the next 11 sts, SM)6x
Continue in this way until all 4 rounds of the **Baby Shale Stitch** pattern are completed.
Repeat these 4 rounds **2x** more - for a total of **3 repeats** (**12 rounds** total).

{Large size}
First round: (k2, **Baby Shale Stitch** over the next 11 sts, k1, PM)5x across round.
Next round: (k2, follow the next round of the **Baby Shale Stitch** over the next 13 sts, k1, SM)5x
Continue in this way until all 4 rounds of the **Baby Shale Stitch** pattern are completed.
Repeat these 4 rounds **2x** more - for a total of **3 repeats** (**12 rounds** total).

2. Ribbing:

Decrease **2 sts** evenly on the next round, as follows: (**64**){**68**} sts total after decrease.
N1 *(n1/n2)* - k1, skp, knit to end of needle
N2 *(n3/n4)* - k1, k2tog, knit to end of needle

Next round: (k2, p2) around all needles
Repeat this ribbing round 4 more times - **5 rounds** total.

Knit and rearrange sts on the next round:

[(k2, p2)6x, k1] on the first needle(s), **N1** *(n1/n2)* = **25 sts** *(for both sizes)* and [k1, (p2, k2)(**9x**){**10x**}, p2] on second needle(s), **N2** *(n3/n4)* = (**39**){**43**} **sts.**

3. Leg:

Set-up Round:
N1 *(n1/n2)* **-** (k2, p2) 6x, k1
N2 *(n3/n4)* **-** m1, k1, (p2, k2)(**9x**){**10x**}, p2 =(**40**){**44**} **sts**

Round 1:
N1 *(n1/n2)* - Follow **Daisy Lace** pattern over **25 sts**
N2 *(n3/n4)* - (k2, p2)(**10x**){**11x**}

Repeat this round for **2 repeats** of the **Daisy Lace** pattern = **2.5"/6.35 cm each Round** or **5"/12.7 cm** and **48 rounds** total. You will now have (**65**){**69**} **sts total**.

4. Preparation for Heel Flap:

On **N1** *(n1)*, (k2, p2)2x. Move these **8 sts** to the back needle, **N2** *(n4)*. Back on **N1** again, (k2, p2), follow **Row 1** of the **Daisy Lace** pattern over the next 25 sts, then transfer **4 sts**

from the back needle, **N2** *(n3)* to **N1** *(n2)* and (k2, p2) over those 4 transferred sts. At this point, you will have (**33**){**33**} **sts** on **N1** *(n1/n2)* [From now on, this will be the **INSTEP** of the sock] and (**32**){**36**} **sts** on **N2** *(n3/n4)* [From now on, this will be the **HEEL** of the sock].

5. Heel Flap:

Working with **N2** *(n3/n4)* aka the **Heel** section, you will now be turning the work for every row, instead of working in rounds. You will ONLY be working on **N2** *(n3/n4)* for this section. The instep needle(s) **N1** *(n1/n2)* will "rest" until you've completed the heel flap, heel turn and gusset.

(Right side/outside of sock will be facing you.)
First Set-up Row: skp, (p2, k2)(7x){8x}, k2tog
Next Set-up Row: sl1(purlwise), (p2, k2)(7x){8x}, k1

You will now have (**30**){**34**} **sts** on the heel flap needle.

Continue with:

Row 1: s1(purlwise), (p2, k2)(7x){8x}, k1
Row 2: sl1(purlwise), (p2, k2)(7x){8x}, k1
Repeat Rows 1 and 2 until heel flap measures **2"/5 cm** or desired height, approximately **16 rows** total *(after set-up rows)*. Continue with the **Heel Turn.**

6. Heel Turn:

Row 1: sl1, k(16){18}, k2tog, k1. Turn.
Row 2: sl1, p5, p2tog, p1. Turn.
Row 3: sl1, k6, k2tog, k1. Turn.
Row 4: sl1, p7, p2tog, p1. Turn.
Row 5: sl1, k8, k2tog, k1. Turn.

Row 6: sl1, p9, p2tog, p1. Turn.
Row 7: sl1, k10, k2tog, k1. Turn.
Row 8: sl1, p11, p2tog, p1. Turn.
Row 9: sl1, k12, k2tog, k1. Turn.
Row 10: sl1, p13, p2tog, p1. Turn.
Row 11: sl1, k14, k2tog, k1. Turn.
Row 12: sl1, p15, p2tog, p1. Turn. (*medium size* ends.)
Row 13: sl1, k16, k2tog, k1. Turn.
Row 14: sl1, p15, p2tog, p1. Turn.
Row 15: sl1, k16, k2tog, k1. Turn.
Row 16: sl1, p17, p2tog, p1. Turn. (*large size* ends.)

The heel is now complete. You will have (**18**){**20**} **sts** remaining on **N2** (*n3/n4*).

7. Preparation for the Gusset:

Continuing on **N2** (*n3/n4*):

Sl1, k(17){19}, pick up and knit 10 sts in the slipped sts of the heel flap plus an additional stitch in the corner - **11 sts total** picked up and knit.

Switch to **N1** (*n1/n2*):

(k2, p2), resume with Row 2 of the **Daisy Lace** pattern, (k2, p2)

With **N2** (*n3*)

Pick up 1 stitch in the corner plus **10 sts** in the slipped stitch side of the heel flap, k(9){10} - **11 sts total** picked up and knit. (*For **Magic Loop** and **2 Circs**, place a beginning-of-the-round marker here. With **dpns**, clip a stitch marker to the very last stitch on this needle, n3.*)

8. Gusset:

Note: Round 1 begins in the <u>middle</u> of N2 (or beginning of n4). The decrease section will start at the end of N2 (n4).

Round 1:
Beginning on **N2** (*n4*): k to 4 sts before the end, k2tog, k2.

On **N1** (*n1/n2*): (k2, p2), continue with next row of the **Daisy Lace** pattern (*should be Row 3*), (k2, p2).
On **N2** (*n3*): k2, ssk, knit to the end of the needle.

Round 2:
N2 (*n4*): knit all sts
N1 (*n1/n2*): (k2, p2), continue with the next row of the **Daisy Lace** pattern, (k2, p2). (*This round for the **Daisy Lace** pattern should just be knit.*)
N2 (*n3*): knit all sts

Repeat Rounds 1 and 2 until (**32**){**34**} **sts** remain on **N2** (*n3/n4*). You should have (**33**){**33**} **sts** on **N1** (*n1/n2*).

9. Foot:

Continue the pattern on the instep (*over **33 sts***) as previously stated: (k2, p2), **Daisy Lace** pattern over 25 sts, (k2, p2) on **N1** (*n1/n2*) and knitting every round on **N2** (*n3/n4*) on the **34 sts** of the foot (*previously heel*) section. Total sts on all needles: (**65**) {**67**} sts.

For women's medium shoe size 8 (**9.5"/24.1 cm**) foot length, follow this pattern until the foot measures **7.5"/19 cm**, from the heel. For a shoe size/ longer foot length, continue with this pattern until the foot section measures **2.25"/5.72 cm less** than desired foot length (*this might require extra yarn if foot length is longer than 10.5"/26.7 cm*).

10. Toe:

When foot section is close to the desired length, (decrease) {increase} 1 st on **N1** *(n1)* on the next round before beginning toe decreases. *(This creates an even number of sts on **N1** & **N2**.)*

Begin the toe decreases as follows -

Round 1:
N1 *(n1/n2)*: k2, ssk, knit to 4 sts before end of needle, k2tog, k2
N2 *(n3/n4)*: same as **N1**

Round 2:
Knit across entire round on all needles.

Repeat Rounds 1 and 2 until a total of **20 sts** remain on the needles. Use Kitchener Stitch to close the toe together, neatly. Cut yarn, leaving an **3-4"/7.6-10.1 cm** tail to weave in later. Follow **Finishing** directions below for both socks.

Directions *(**LEFT** sock)*

Follow directions for **RIGHT** sock until the beginning of the **48th round.**

4. Preparation for Heel Flap:

After following the **Daisy Lace** pattern on **N1** *(n1/n2)*, (k2, p2)6x on **N2** *(n3)* and move the next **16 sts** onto **N1**. With **N1** *(n1/n2)*, (k2, p2), pm, then follow Row 1 of the **Daisy Lace** pattern over the next **25 sts**, pm, (k2, p2). Transfer the remaining **8 sts** to **N2** *(n3)* At this point, you will have (**33**){**33**} **sts** on **N1** *(n1/n2)* [From now on, this will be the **INSTEP** section of the sock] and (**32**){**36**} **sts** on **N2** *(n3/n4)* [From now on, this will be the **HEEL** section of the sock].

After finishing the **Preparation for Heel Flap**, continue with the **Heel Flap** directions for the **RIGHT** sock until the **LEFT** sock is complete. Continue to **Finishing**.

11. Finishing:

Weave in all ends, neatly, on the inside of the sock. You may wish to lightly steam the socks *(under a press cloth)* to open up the lace a bit or soak & spin dry socks and place on sock blockers (or lay flat) until completely dry.

About Blocking Lace

So, what is blocking exactly?

After knitting and completing a lace project, blocking means more than one thing:

- washing your newly finished knitted piece
- gently stretching, readjusting and assisting the stitches in your knitted piece to your desired dimensions
- smoothing out your stitches so they will lay properly
- helping to give your knitted item a more finished, professional look

How do I block my lace item when it's finished?

There are various ways that you can accomplish this:

- soak your piece in a gentle, fiber safe wash (Eucalan, Soak, etc.) in the appropriate temperature water (usually tepid is safe) for at least a few hours or overnight
- remember NOT to twist and mangle the knitted item when rinsing, but to hold it carefully and supporting the weight of it in your hands when it is saturated with water.
- roll your item in a large, thick, dry towel and press out all of the excess water OR store it safely in a lingerie bag and place in the *spin cycle only* of your washer
- lay out and pin your knitted piece to dry on large bed, foam blocking squares or other flat surface, using blocking pins or wires or both
- *occasionally* steam from your iron can work on some items

 Links to **excellent, helpful articles** about blocking:

http://knitty.com/ISSUEwinter02/FEATdiyknitter.html
http://www.purlbee.com/blocking-tutorial/
http://www.yarnharlot.ca/blog/archives/2005/08/23/walk_around_the_block.html
http://techknitting.blogspot.com/2008/03/why-block-hand-knits-heres-why-and-how.html
http://knitting.about.com/od/finishingtouches/a/blocking-lace.htm

 Links to **favorite websites** for lace accessories & yarn:

http://www.knitpicks.com
http://www.morehousefarm.com
http://www.patternworks.com
http://www.covetedyarn.com
http://www.yarn.com
https://www.tessyarns.com
http://www.etsy.com
http://madcolorfiberarts.com
http://www.purlsoho.com/purl

Favorite **local yarn stores** to check out:

The Elegant Ewe (Concord, NH), **The Spotted Sheep Shoppe** (Goffstown, NH), **The Knitting Knook** (Keene, NH), **The Yarn and Fiber Company** (Derry, NH), **The Knitting Studio** (Montpelier, VT), **The Yarn Sellar** (York, ME), **Hub Mills** (N.Billerica, MA), **Coveted Yarn** (Gloucester, MA), **Tess' Designer Yarns** (Portland, ME), **Spunky Eclectic** (Lisbon, ME), **Patternworks** (C.Harbor, NH) **Fiber Studio** (Henniker, NH) & **Northeast Fiber Art** (Williston, VT)

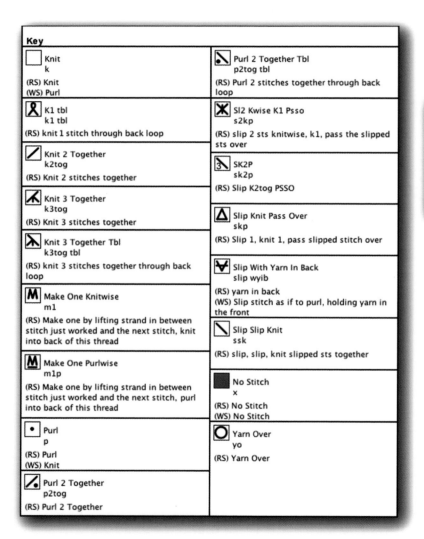

Key

Knit k (RS) Knit (WS) Purl	**Purl 2 Together Tbl** p2tog tbl (RS) Purl 2 stitches together through back loop
K1 tbl k1 tbl (RS) knit 1 stitch through back loop	**Sl2 Kwise K1 Psso** s2kp (RS) slip 2 sts knitwise, k1, pass the slipped sts over
Knit 2 Together k2tog (RS) Knit 2 stitches together	**SK2P** sk2p (RS) Slip K2tog PSSO
Knit 3 Together k3tog (RS) Knit 3 stitches together	**Slip Knit Pass Over** skp (RS) Slip 1, knit 1, pass slipped stitch over
Knit 3 Together Tbl k3tog tbl (RS) knit 3 stitches together through back loop	**Slip With Yarn In Back** slip wyib (RS) yarn in back (WS) Slip stitch as if to purl, holding yarn in the front
Make One Knitwise m1 (RS) Make one by lifting strand in between stitch just worked and the next stitch, knit into back of this thread	**Slip Slip Knit** ssk (RS) slip, slip, knit slipped sts together
Make One Purlwise m1p (RS) Make one by lifting strand in between stitch just worked and the next stitch, purl into back of this thread	**No Stitch** x (RS) No Stitch (WS) No Stitch
Purl p (RS) Purl (WS) Knit	**Yarn Over** yo (RS) Yarn Over
Purl 2 Together p2tog (RS) Purl 2 Together	

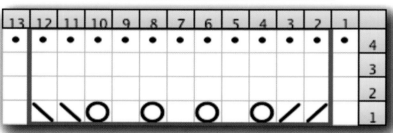

Repeat pattern in **BLUE**.

Baby Shale Stitch: *(11 stitch repeat)*

Round 1: (k2tog)2x, (yo, k1)3x, yo, (ssk)2x
Rounds 2 and 3: knit
Round 4: purl

Daisy Lace: *(25 stitch pattern repeat)*

Round 1: k1, skp, k3, yo, k1, yo, k3, k2tog, k1, skp, k3, yo, k1, yo, k3, k2tog, k1

Round 2 and all even rounds: knit

Round 3: k1, skp, k2, yo, k3, yo, k2, k2tog, k1, skp, k2, yo, k3, yo, k2, k2tog, k1

Round 5: k1, yo, skp, k1, yo, skp, k1, k2tog, yo, k1, k2tog, yo, k1, yo, skp, k1, yo, skp, k1, k2tog, yo, k1, k2tog, yo, k1

Round 7: k2, yo, skp, k1, yo, s2kp, yo, k1, k2tog, yo, k3, yo, skp, k1, yo, s2kp, yo, k1, k2tog, yo, k2

Round 9: k1, (yo, skp)2x, k3, k2tog, yo, k2tog, yo, k1, (yo, skp)2x, k3, (k2tog, yo)2x, k1

Round 11: k2, (yo, skp)2x, k1, (k2tog, yo)2x, k3, (yo, skp)2x, k1, (k2tog, yo)2x, k2

Round 13: k1, yo, k3, k2tog, k1, skp, k3, yo, k1, yo, k3, k2tog, k1, skp, k3, yo, k1

Round 15: k2, yo, k2, k2tog, k1, skp, k2, yo, k3, yo, k2, k2tog, k1, skp, k2, yo, k2

Round 17: k1, (k2tog, yo, k1)2x, (yo, skp, k1)2x, (k2tog, yo, k1)2x, (yo, skp, k1)2x

Round 19: (k2tog, yo, k1)2x, k2, yo, skp, k1, yo, sk2p, yo, k1, k2tog, yo, k2, (k1, yo, skp)2x

Round 21: k2, (k2tog, yo)2x, k1, (yo, skp)2x, k3, (k2tog, yo)2x, k1, (yo, skp)2x, k2

Round 23: k1, (k2tog, yo)2x, k3, (yo, skp)2x, k1, (k2tog, yo)2x, k3, (yo, skp)2x, k1

Round 24: knit

Repeat Rounds 1-24 for pattern.

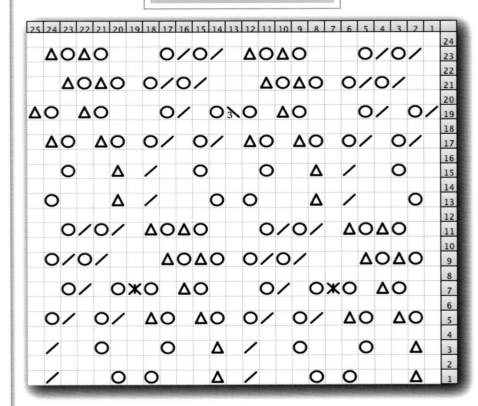

Daisy Lace

Megaera Mitts

Named for one of the Greek "Furies", these extra long mitts feature a leaf lace pattern that closely resembles burning flames of justice. In contrast to the frightening appearance of this goddess, the mitts are knit using a soft pink yarn to remind the world of love and beauty. While this goddess is inflexible, the ribbing section is extremely flexible and forms perfectly to your arm. This pattern of contradiction creates mitts that are supremely soft and enjoyable to wear.

Pattern Difficulty:

Yarn:
(1) 1.76 oz/50 g skein (136 yds/124.4 m) of **Knit Picks**
Sugarbunny (80% merino/20% angora) in "melon" OR
{1} 3.5 oz/100 g skein (210 yds/192 m) of **Malabrigo** *Worsted*
(100% merino) in "buscando azul #186" .

Both sizes used approximately **115 yards/105.2 m** of yarn.

Needle: US 5 (4mm) in either a 32-40"/81.2 - 101.6 cm circular
for Magic Loop (or a set of 5 dpns) or needle size necessary to
obtain gauge

Gauge:
(small/medium) **5.5** sts and **7** rows = 1"/2.5 cm (stockinette)
{*large*} **5** sts and **6.5** rows = 1"/2.5 cm (stockinette)

Notions: clip on stitch marker *(or safety pin)*, stitch markers,
scissors, measuring tape, tapestry needle, (3/8"/.95 cm) 56"/
142.2 cm long gauze ribbon *(or ribbon style of choice)*, row counter,
stitch holder or 12"/30.5 cm length of waste yarn for holding
thumb stitches.

Finished Size:
(women's hand & wrist circumference)
small/medium (**7.75"** & **6"**/*19.7 cm & 15.2 cm*)
large {**8.75** & **7"**/*21.6 cm & 17.8 cm*}

NOTE: You will be using the same size needle to knit the mitts
of each size, but using different weight yarns to vary the size.
The small/medium size uses a **DK** yarn and the large uses a
worsted/heavy worsted yarn. The mitts can easily be made
with the ribbon or without, depending on your style. The mitts
for each hand are knit exactly the same, the front and back of
the mitts are identical.

Directions *(make 2)*

1. Cuff:

Being careful not to twist, CO **40** sts. Clip a stitch marker to the
very first stitch to denote the beginning of the round. *(as you
continue to knit the mitt, you should occasionally move the clipped st marker
up to the appropriate stitch above)*

(k1, p1) across round until cuff measures **5"**/12.7 cm from
beginning.

2. Preparation for Thumb:

*Option 1 (**no-ribbon**, follow these directions)*

Set up round: k16, PM, (k1, p1)4x, PM, k16
Repeat Set up round: k16, (k1, p1)4x, k16
Next round: k1, follow **Triple Leaf Lace** pattern over 15
sts, (k1, p1)4x, k1, follow **Triple Leaf Lace** pattern over the
next 15 stitches *(slipping markers as you go along)*.
Repeat the "next round" until the section above the cuff
ribbing measures **2"**/5 cm, or entire mitt from cast on measures
7"/17.8 cm total.

*Option 2 (**with ribbon**, follow these directions)*

Set up round: (k2tog, yo) across round
Knit 1 round
Next round: k1, follow **Triple Leaf Lace** pattern over 15
sts, PM, (k1, p1)4x, PM, k1, follow **Triple Leaf Lace** pattern
over the next 15 stitches *(slipping markers as you go along)*.
Repeat the "next round" until this section above the cuff
ribbing measures **2"**/5 cm, or entire mitt from cast on measures
7"/17.8 cm total. You should be able to complete an entire **12
row repeat** of the lace pattern in the **2"**/5 cm.

For **BOTH** options, continue onto the "**Hand Section**" directions.

3. Hand Section:

K1, follow **Triple Leaf Lace** pattern, place 8 sts on a stitch holder or waste yarn, PM, cast on 8 stitches *(snugly)* over the gap, PM, k1, follow **Triple Leaf Lace** pattern.

Continue with the directions below until 2 full repeats of the **Triple Leaf Lace** pattern are completed - **24** rounds total:

(k1, follow **Triple Leaf Lace** pattern)2x, slipping st markers as you go.

Complete the hand section of the mitt with 3 rounds of (k1, p1) ribbing.

BO all stitches *(in pattern)* snugly. Cut yarn, leaving at least a **4"**/10 cm tail for weaving in.

4. Thumb Section:

Place the **8** thumb sts onto a needle. Clip the beginning of round marker to the right most st on the needle. With another needle and yarn, pick up and knit **1** st from the corner of the opening. With the same needle, pick up **6** sts along the cast on edge of the hand of the mitt. Then, with this same needle, pick up and knit one more st at the corner of the opening. You should now have **8** sts on the first needle and **8** sts on the second - **16 sts** total. (k1, p1)8x across round. Repeat this 1x1 ribbing for **6** more rounds or until desired thumb length. BO in pattern. Cut yarn, leaving at least a **4"**/10 cm tail for weaving in.

5. Adding ribbon:

Cut the ribbon in half, so that you have TWO 28"/71.1 cm lengths of ribbon...one for each mitt. Starting at the side exactly **opposite** to the thumb of the mitt, thread the end of the ribbon down into one of the holes. Bring the ribbon up through the next hole. Continue in this fashion until you reach the point where you started. You should end with the ribbon coming up out of a hole so that you have both ends of the ribbon dangling off the side of the mitt. You may wish tie the ribbon loosely before putting it on your hand and then tighten the bow after you've got the mitt where you want it.

6. Finishing:

Weave in all ends, neatly. You may wish to lightly steam the mitts *(under a press cloth)* to open up the lace a bit.

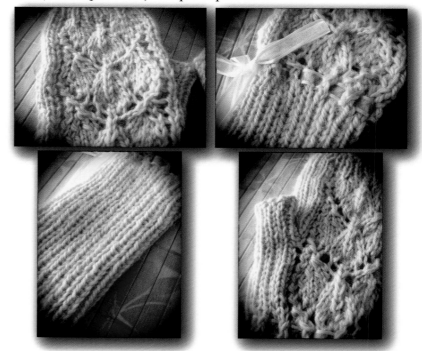

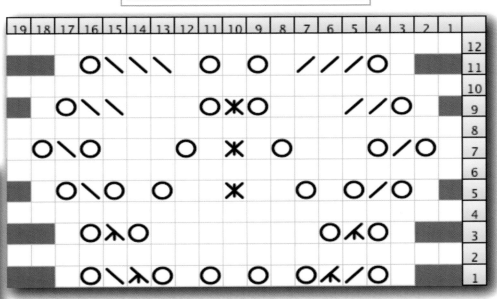

{large size}
in
worsted
weight yarn

Triple Leaf Lace

Key

Knit k (RS) Knit (WS) Purl	Purl 2 Together Tbl p2tog tbl (RS) Purl 2 stitches together through back loop
K1 tbl k1 tbl (RS) knit 1 stitch through back loop	Sl2 Kwise K1 Psso s2kp (RS) slip 2 sts knitwise, k1, pass the slipped sts over
Knit 2 Together k2tog (RS) Knit 2 stitches together	SK2P sk2p (RS) Slip K2tog PSSO
Knit 3 Together k3tog (RS) Knit 3 stitches together	Slip Knit Pass Over skp (RS) Slip 1, knit 1, pass slipped stitch over
Knit 3 Together Tbl k3tog tbl (RS) knit 3 stitches together through back loop	Slip With Yarn In Back slip wyib (RS) yarn in back (WS) Slip stitch as if to purl, holding yarn in the front
Make One Knitwise m1 (RS) Make one by lifting strand in between stitch just worked and the next stitch, knit into back of this thread	Slip Slip Knit ssk (RS) slip, slip, knit slipped sts together
Make One Purlwise m1p (RS) Make one by lifting strand in between stitch just worked and the next stitch, purl into back of this thread	No Stitch x (RS) No Stitch (WS) No Stitch
Purl p (RS) Purl (WS) Knit	Yarn Over yo (RS) Yarn Over
Purl 2 Together p2tog (RS) Purl 2 Together	

Triple Leaf Lace: *(15 stitch repeat)*

Round 1 (rs): k1, yo, k2tog, k3tog, (yo, k1)3x, yo, k3togtbl, ssk, yo, k1
Round 2 and all even rounds: knit
Round 3: k1, yo, k3tog, yo, k7, yo, k3togtbl, yo, k1
Round 5: k1, yo, k2tog, yo, k1, yo, k2, s2kp, k2, yo, k1, yo, ssk, yo, k1
Round 7: k1, yo, k2tog, yo, k3, yo, k1, s2kp, k1, yo, k3, yo, ssk, yo, k1
Round 9: k1, yo, (k2tog)2x, k3, yo, s2kp, yo, k3, (ssk)2x, yo, k1
Round 11: k1, yo, (k2tog)3x, (k1, yo)2x, k1, (ssk)3x, yo, k1
Round 12: knit

Repeat Rounds 1-12 for pattern.

Hunter Scarf

Picture the Huntsman from "*Snow White and the Seven Dwarves*" wearing this masculine style scarf, which is not only very handsome, but also warm. The use of a heathered, self-striping yarn in combination with lace stitches gives the scarf added depth and texture. The width and length of this scarf can be easily adapted. The lace pattern isn't difficult with only 2 actual lace rows - making this a perfect first lace project.

Pattern Difficulty:

Yarn:
(3) 1.76 oz/50 g skeins (108 yds/98.7 m each) of **Noro** *Kureyon*
   (100% wool) in "#236A" OR
(**324 yards**/296.3 m or 5.29 oz/150 g) of 100% wool, self-
striping aran yarn

Needle: US **8** (5 mm), straight or circular or needle size
necessary to obtain gauge

Gauge: **4** sts and **8** rows = 1"/2.5 cm (garter)
          3.5 sts and **4** rows = 1"/2.5 cm (lace)

Notions: tapestry needle, scissors, measuring tape, stitch
markers *(optional, use as needed)*

Finished Size: 8.25"/21 cm wide x **54"**/137.2 cm long *(unblocked)*

Directions

CO **30** sts, loosely.
Knit 2 rows

1. Body of scarf:

Row 1 *(rs)*: (sl 1, k2), follow **Vertical Lace Trellis** pattern to
last 10 sts, k10
Row 2 *(ws)*: (sl 1, k9), purl to last 3 sts, k3

Repeat Rows 1 and 2 until scarf is **53.5"**/135.9 cm long from
beginning *(approximately **100 repeats** of the 4 row **Vertical Lace
Trellis** pattern)*, ending with a RS row *(or Row 1)*.

Knit 2 rows.

BO all stitches. Weave in ends.

2. Finishing:

You may not wish to block this scarf *(it has a great texture without
blocking)*, but if you do, I'd recommend lightly steaming the scarf
on the wrong side using a steam iron about **2"**/5 cm away from
the scarf or on top of cotton press cloth.

Key

Knit k (RS) Knit (WS) Purl	**Purl 2 Together Tbl** p2tog tbl (RS) Purl 2 stitches together through back loop
K1 tbl k1 tbl (RS) knit 1 stitch through back loop	**Sl2 Kwise K1 Psso** s2kp (RS) slip 2 sts knitwise, k1, pass the slipped sts over
Knit 2 Together k2tog (RS) Knit 2 stitches together	**SK2P** sk2p (RS) Slip K2tog PSSO
Knit 3 Together k3tog (RS) Knit 3 stitches together	**Slip Knit Pass Over** skp (RS) Slip 1, knit 1, pass slipped stitch over
Knit 3 Together Tbl k3tog tbl (RS) knit 3 stitches together through back loop	**Slip With Yarn In Back** slip wyib (RS) yarn in back (WS) Slip stitch as if to purl, holding yarn in the front
Make One Knitwise m1 (RS) Make one by lifting strand in between stitch just worked and the next stitch, knit into back of this thread	**Slip Slip Knit** ssk (RS) slip, slip, knit slipped sts together
Make One Purlwise m1p (RS) Make one by lifting strand in between stitch just worked and the next stitch, purl into back of this thread	**No Stitch** x (RS) No Stitch (WS) No Stitch
Purl p (RS) Purl (WS) Knit	**Yarn Over** yo (RS) Yarn Over
Purl 2 Together p2tog (RS) Purl 2 Together	

Vertical Lace Trellis

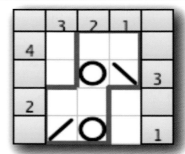

Repeat pattern in **BLUE.**

Vertical Lace Trellis:
(over an odd number of sts)

Rows 1 *(rs)*: k1, *yo, k2tog; repeat from * to end
Rows 2 & 4 *(ws)*: purl
Rows 3: *ssk, yo; repeat from * to last st, k1

Repeat Rows 1-4 for pattern.

La Bête Pillows

These lovely pillows are not only enjoyable to knit, they are also soft and fluffy, reminding me of an elegantly dressed **Beast** (or La Bête, in French). They can be knit using whatever color(s) you wish - to match your living room, bedroom or any special place in your home. This pattern uses a different color for the trim bind off, but you could also use the main color instead. Covering the pillow forms with pretty fabric in a contrasting color really makes these pillows unique and attractive for any room in the house.

Pattern Difficulty:

Yarn:
(2) 3.5 oz/100 g skeins (110 yds/100 m) of **Knit Picks** *Biggo* (50% superwash merino/50% nylon) in "Reindeer Heather" (or "Woodland Heather") and (1) skein in "Sapphire Heather"

Needle:
(2) US **11** (6 mm) needles 24"/61 cm circular and
(1) US **11** (6 mm) straight or needle size necessary to obtain gauge

Gauge: **3** sts and **3.5** rows = 1"/2.5 cm (stockinette)

Notions: 6 large stitch markers, 16"/41 cm pillow form, scissors, tapestry needle, row counter, 4 extra large stitch holders or waste yarn for holding live stitches before binding off, tape measure and *(optional)* 2 fat quarters (18" x 22"/45.7 x 55.8 cm) of cotton quilting fabric in a contrasting design/color, matching sewing thread, sewing machine *(or sewing needle for hand stitching)*

Finished Size: 16" x **16"**/40.6 cm x 40.6 cm *(unblocked)*

NOTE: Each pillow used a total of approximately **220 yards/ 201 m** of yarn in the main color and **10 yards/9 m** of the contrast color = **230 yards/210 m** total of a bulky yarn.

Directions *(for EACH pillow)*

1. Pillow Face: *(make 2*)*

CO **47** sts with one of the circular needles.

Row 1: (sl1, k1), pm, follow the **Daisies and Ladders Lace** pattern over the next 13 sts, pm, k2, pm, follow the **Daisies and Ladders Lace** pattern over the next 13 sts, pm, k2, pm, follow the **Daisies and Ladders Lace** pattern over the next 13 sts, pm, k2.

Row 2: sl1, purl to the end, slipping st markers as you go.

Repeat **Rows 1 & 2** *one more time.* On the third repeat of the **Daisies and Ladders Lace** pattern, ending with **Row 17**, removing st markers as you go along. Keep the sts on the needle and cut the yarn, leaving a 3-4"/7.6-10 cm tail.

*Make the second pillow the same as the first, but **DO NOT** cut the yarn. Continue with "Joining the Pillow Faces".

2. Joining the Pillow Faces:

After both pillow faces are complete (with sts still on the needles), you are ready to join 3 out of the 4 sides together.

To join the **TOP** of the pillow together, follow these directions:

With wrong sides together, place both pillow faces in front of you, with the live sts on the top and needles parallel. The tips of the needles should point to the right *(adjust if this is not the case)*. Using the straight needle and the contrasting yarn for the trim, begin the three needle bind off process as follows:

Place the working needle into the first st on BOTH needles as if to knit and knit both sts together at the same time. Repeat. There will be two sts on the right hand needle and you will pass the second st over the first. Continue in this fashion until all sts have been bound off. Cut yarn *(leaving a 3-4"/7.6-10 cm tail)* and pull through last st.

To join the **SIDE,** follow these directions:

Now, separate your contrasting color trim yarn into <u>2 equal balls</u>.

Turn the pillow face 1/4 turn to the left. *(The top side you just finished will be on your left.)* With one circular needle *(and RS facing you)* pick up and knit 47 sts along the pillow face with one of the balls of yarn. Repeat on the other side with the other ball of yarn and circular needle. Adjust the needles so that both tips are facing to the right. With the straight needle, follow the three needle bind off process described above.

Repeat this again for the **BOTTOM** part of the pillow.

3. Pillowcase Covers: *(optional, but recommended)*

Wash and press your selected fabric. Cut 2 pieces (per pillow) of fabric **16 3/4" x 16 3/4"**/42.5 x 42.5 cm. Using a **1/4"**/.64 cm seam allowance and placing the right sides of the fabric together, sew a straight seam along 3 out of the 4 edges of the fabric, pivoting at each corner. Press your pillow case cover again, paying attention to the corners. Also, press the open side's **1/4"**/.64 cm seam allowance to the inside of the pillowcase.

Place your pillow form inside the case and, using matching thread, use an invisible mattress stitch to sew up the last side.

(See **Figure A**)

4. Finishing the Pillows:

When the pillow form is covered, place the finished pillow inside of the knitted pillowcase. Follow the directions for the **SIDE** joining of the pillow faces. (See **Figure A**) Using the leftover contrasting trim yarn and tapestry needle, join the 2 sides at each corner of the pillow faces to connect and knot tightly. Weave in all ends neatly on the wrong side of the pillowcase.

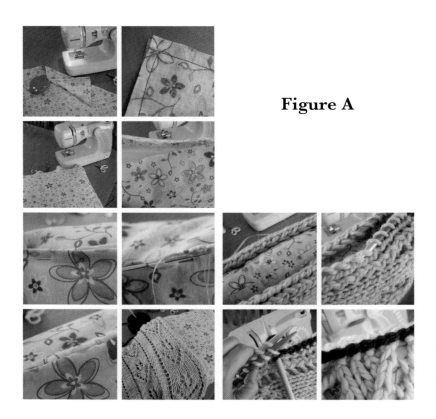

Figure A

Daisies and Ladders Lace: *(13 stitch pattern repeat)*

Row 1 (RS): skp, yo, k3, k2tog, yo, k4, yo, k2tog
Row 2 *(and all even rows)***:** purl
Row 3: skp, yo, k2, k2tog, yo, k1, yo, skp, k2, yo, k2tog
Row 5: skp, yo, k1, k2tog, yo, k3, yo, skp, k1, yo, k2tog
Row 7: skp, yo, k2tog, yo, k5, yo, skp, yo, k2tog
Row 9: skp, yo, k2, k2tog, yo, ktbl, yo, skp, k2, yo, k2tog
Row 11: skp, yo, k3, s2kp, yo, k3, yo, k2tog
Row 13: skp, yo, k2, skp, yo, ktbl, yo, k2tog, k2, yo, k2tog
Row 15: skp, yo, k9, yo, k2tog
Row 17: skp, yo, k9, yo, k2tog
Row 18: purl

Repeat Rows 1-18 for pattern.

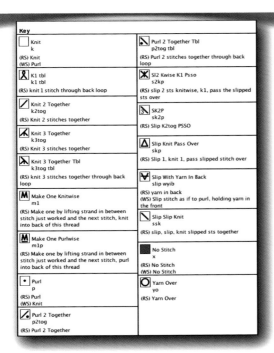

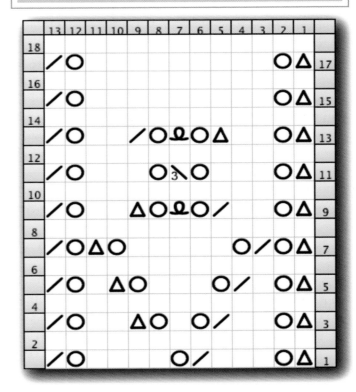

Daisies and Ladders Lace

Veronica Earrings

A super light, airy and delicate earring pattern that is quick to knit and delightful to wear. Only a small amount of yarn is needed for this project, which can be knit using any laceweight yarn - solid & variegated colorways look great. The name of these earrings was inspired by the author of a book that I love, *"Little Book of Fairy Tales"* by Veronica Uribe. For some reason, I can picture her wearing these as she writes these classic, childhood tales. Use your imagination with this pattern - you could even knit a few leaves and make a beautiful necklace to match your earrings.

Pattern Difficulty:

Yarn:

(1) 1.8 oz/50 g skein (740 yds/676.7 m) of **Nandia** *Cashmere Silk Blend* (45% cashmere/55% silk) in "black". These earrings used approximately **2 yards**/1.8 m of yarn.

Needle: US **0** (2 mm) straights or dpns *(I recommend dpns - they're easier to work with.)* or needle size necessary to obtain gauge

Gauge: **10** sts and **12** rows = 1"/2.5 cm (stockinette stitch)

Notions: 2 small ball hooked earring findings, small needle nose jewelry pliers, scissors, tapestry needle, measuring tape

Finished Size: **1.25"** x **0.75"**/3.2 cm tall x 1.9 cm wide at the widest point of the earring *(blocked)*

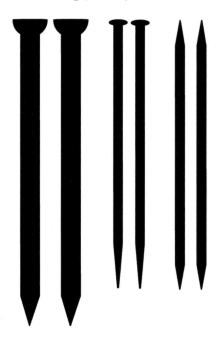

Directions *(make 2)*

1. Body of Earring:

CO 9 sts.

Follow the **Leaf Lace** pattern until Row 15.

Cut yarn, leaving a **3"**/7.6 cm tail. Pull tail through last stitch to secure.

2. Finishing:

Weave in all ends neatly. To block, place right side down onto a flat, heat proof surface, cover with a press cloth and lightly steam. Remove press cloth, turn right side up and pin gently to open up the lace pattern.

Adding Earring Finding: *(it's MUCH easier than it sounds, really.)*

Begin by holding the earring finding with the hook on top and the loop at the bottom *(making sure that the tiny gap between the hook and the small loop is facing up)*. Then, using the pliers, gently grab the loop with the tips of the pliers and make a larger opening between the hook and the loop <u>by twisting the tips of the pliers and the edge of the loop AWAY from you</u>, **NOT** by pulling the loop out to the side *(this weakens the integrity of the finding)*.

Now, hold the knitted earring *(with wrong side facing the same way as the tip of the earring that goes through your ear and the point of the earring facing down)* next to the opening in the loop that you just created. Using that enlarged opening as a mini "hook", grab a strand or two of yarn in the very middle center of the earring *(where the earring forms a heart shape)*.

When you have the earring placed exactly where you want it, use the pliers to gently pull the edge of the loop back towards you into place. You might have to use the pliers to also squeeze the edge of the loop and the base of the hook together for better closure. Follow this same procedure with the second earring. (See **Figure A**)

Figure A

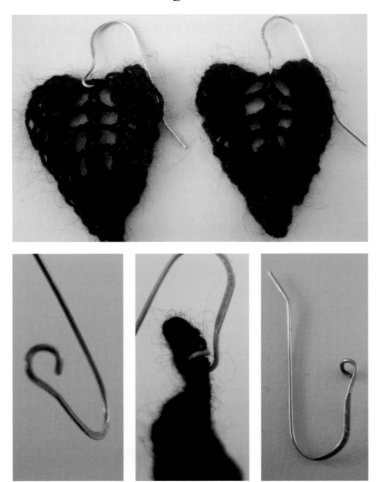

Lace Leaf Pattern:

Row 1 *(rs)*: k2, k2tog, yo, k1, yo, skp, k2
Row 2 *(ws)* **and all even rows to 14:** purl
Row 3: k1, k2tog, k1, yo, k1, yo, k1, skp, k1
Row 5: k2tog, k2, yo, k1, yo, k2, skp
Row 7: skp, k2, yo, k1, yo, k2, k2tog
Row 9: k1, skp, k3, k2tog, k1
Row 11: k1, skp, k1, k2tog k1
Row 13: k1, s2kp, k1
Row 15: s2kp

Key

☐ Knit k (RS) Knit (WS) Purl	↘ Purl 2 Together Tbl p2tog tbl (RS) Purl 2 stitches together through back loop
⋊ K1 tbl k1 tbl (RS) knit 1 stitch through back loop	✳ Sl2 Kwise K1 Psso s2kp (RS) slip 2 sts knitwise, k1, pass the slipped sts over
╱ Knit 2 Together k2tog (RS) Knit 2 stitches together	↘ SK2P sk2p (RS) Slip K2tog PSSO
⋌ Knit 3 Together k3tog (RS) Knit 3 stitches together	△ Slip Knit Pass Over skp (RS) Slip 1, knit 1, pass slipped stitch over
⋋ Knit 3 Together Tbl k3tog tbl (RS) knit 3 stitches together through back loop	⋎ Slip With Yarn In Back slip wyib (RS) yarn in back (WS) Slip stitch as if to purl, holding yarn in the front
Ⓜ Make One Knitwise m1 (RS) Make one by lifting strand in between stitch just worked and the next stitch, knit into back of this thread	↘ Slip Slip Knit ssk (RS) slip, slip, knit slipped sts together
Ⓜ Make One Purlwise m1p (RS) Make one by lifting strand in between stitch just worked and the next stitch, purl into back of this thread	■ No Stitch x (RS) No Stitch (WS) No Stitch
• Purl p (RS) Purl (WS) Knit	Ⓞ Yarn Over yo (RS) Yarn Over
╱ Purl 2 Together p2tog (RS) Purl 2 Together	

Lace Leaf

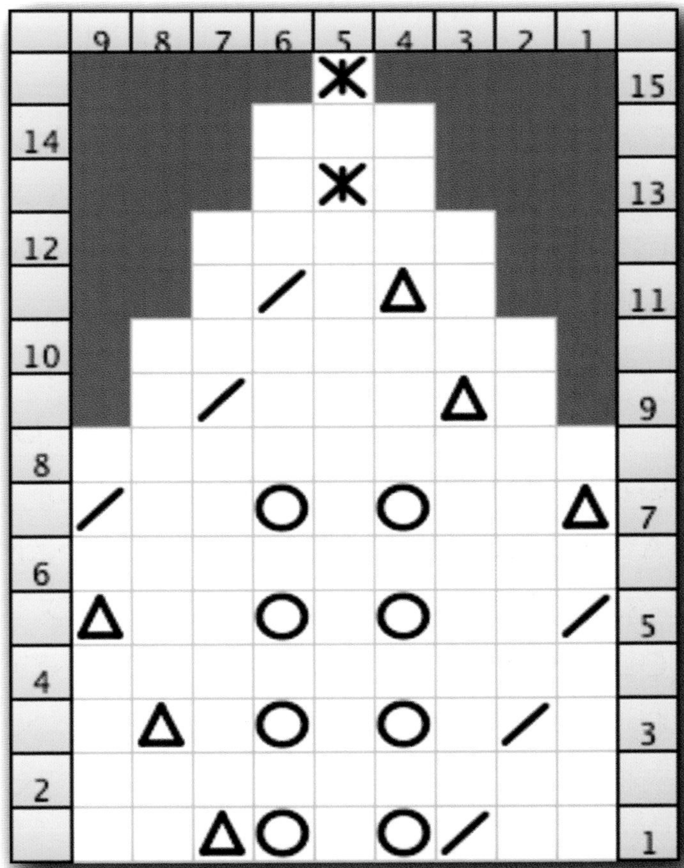

61

Taylor Cowl

This snug, luxurious cowl is perfect for the fall and winter to keep the chills away. Knit using either a dk or bulky yarn, this pattern (named after a dear friend of mine) is also reversible, with a lovely texture on the inside, and so can be worn with either side showing. The Taylor Cowl is a quick, enjoyable knit and the variations are endless. This knit is a perfect gift for someone you love.

Pattern Difficulty:

Yarn:
(DK)

(2) 3.5 oz/100 g skeins (274 yds/250.5 m) of **Mirasol** *Tupa* (50% silk/50% merino wool) in "816" OR

(2) 1.76 oz/50 g skeins (153 yds/140 m) of **Rowan** *Kid Classic* (70% wool, 22% mohair, 8% nylon) in "818"

{*Bulky*}

(2) 3.5 oz/100 g skeins (142 yds/129.8 m) of **Debbie Bliss** *Paloma* (60% baby alpaca/40% merino wool) in "42001"

Needle: US **6**/4mm {**11**/8mm}, 16-24" (40-60 cm) circular or needle size necessary to obtain gauge

Gauge:
(DK)

22 sts and **28** rows = 4"/10 cm (stockinette)

{*Bulky*}

14 sts and **20** rows = 4"/10 cm (stockinette)

Notions: 11 stitch markers, measuring tape, row counter, scissors, tapestry needle

Finished Size:
(DK)

11" x **9"**/28 cm across x 23 cm tall (22"/56 cm around) (*unblocked*)

{*Bulky*}

11" x **8"**/28 cm across x 20 cm tall (22"/56 cm around) (*unblocked*)

Directions

CO **121** sts {**77** *sts*} loosely using long tail cast on. Join in the round, placing a marker and making sure not to twist.

K 1 round
P 1 round
K 1 round

Follow Rounds 1-28 of the **Lacy Waves** pattern. See chart and pattern below. You may wish to add stitch markers after each lace repeat on the first round.

For DK weight yarn only, repeat Rounds 1-28 **one more time.**

Repeat Round 1 of the **Lacy Waves** pattern **3 MORE times**.

P 1 round
K 1 round

BO **loosely** using the following: (p1, *place stitch from the right hand needle onto the left hand needle, p 2 sts together*; repeat from *...* until last stitch). Cut yarn to **4"**/10 cm and pull tail of yarn through last stitch. Weave in ends. Block lightly.

Variations:

Make sure you've done a **gauge swatch** with the yarn and needles you've chosen before tackling *EITHER* variation.

• Making the cowl **smaller or larger:** Decrease or increase number of repeats around - instructions are written for DK (**11 repeats**) and *Bulky* {**7 repeats**} when casting on.

- Making the cowl **shorter or taller:** Increase or decrease the number of lace rounds that you complete - model shown using DK (**56 rounds**) and *Bulky* {**28 rounds**}.

Lacy Waves: *(multiple of 11 sts)*

Round 1: *(rs)* *p1, k10*; repeat *...* across round

Round 2 *(ws)* **and all even rounds:** repeat Round 1

Round 3: repeat Round 1

Rounds 5, 9 & 13: *p1, k1, (yo, k1)3x, (ssk)3x*; repeat *...* across round

Rounds 7 & 11: *p1, k1, (k1, yo)3x, (ssk)3x*; repeat *...* across round

Round 15 & 17: repeat Round 1

Rounds 19, 23 & 27: *p1, (k2tog)3x, (k1, yo)3x, k1*; repeat *...* across round

Rounds 21 & 25: *p1, (k2tog)3x, (yo, k1)2x, yo, k2*: repeat *...* across round

Round 28: repeat Round 1

Repeat Rounds 1-28 for pattern.

(DK) - right side out

(DK) - wrong side out

Lacy Waves

Key

	Knit — k — (RS) Knit — (WS) Purl
⅄	**K1 tbl** — k1 tbl — (RS) knit 1 stitch through back loop
/	**Knit 2 Together** — k2tog — (RS) Knit 2 stitches together
⅄	**Knit 3 Together** — k3tog — (RS) Knit 3 stitches together
⅄	**Knit 3 Together Tbl** — k3tog tbl — (RS) knit 3 stitches together through back loop
M	**Make One Knitwise** — m1 — (RS) Make one by lifting strand in between stitch just worked and the next stitch, knit into back of this thread
M	**Make One Purlwise** — m1p — (RS) Make one by lifting strand in between stitch just worked and the next stitch, purl into back of this thread
•	**Purl** — p — (RS) Purl — (WS) Knit
⁄•	**Purl 2 Together** — p2tog — (RS) Purl 2 Together
⅄	**Purl 2 Together Tbl** — p2tog tbl — (RS) Purl 2 stitches together through back loop
Ⅹ	**Sl2 Kwise K1 Psso** — s2kp — (RS) slip 2 sts knitwise, k1, pass the slipped sts over
⅄	**SK2P** — sk2p — (RS) Slip K2tog PSSO
△	**Slip Knit Pass Over** — skp — (RS) Slip 1, knit 1, pass slipped stitch over
⅄	**Slip With Yarn In Back** — slip wyib — (RS) yarn in back — (WS) Slip stitch as if to purl, holding yarn in the front
⅄	**Slip Slip Knit** — ssk — (RS) slip, slip, knit slipped sts together
■	**No Stitch** — x — (RS) No Stitch — (WS) No Stitch
O	**Yarn Over** — yo — (RS) Yarn Over

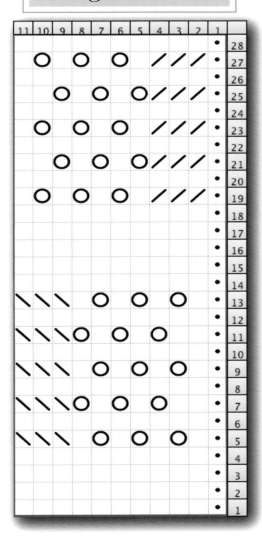

Repeat pattern in **BLUE.**

65

Le Chat Noir Bag

Protect and cherish your favorite tarot deck (or large deck of cards) with this simple lace tarot bag. The black alpaca silk yarn and velvet ribbon closure create a luxurious and practical bag. This hand knit bag would be a thoughtful gift for a tarot enthusiast and looks beautiful in any color.

Pattern Difficulty:

Yarn:

(1) 1.76 oz/50 g skein (146 yds/133 m) of **Blue Sky Alpaca** *Alpaca Silk* (50% alpaca/50% silk) in "black # 150"

Needle: US **3** (3.25 mm) straights and a set of 5 dpns or needle size necessary to obtain gauge. *(I highly recommend using dpns with this project. At each corner of the bag, you will be slipping the first stitch and, if using 4 dpns - one for each side - the corners will be nicely defined.)*

Gauge: **6.5** sts and **8** rows = 1"/2.5 cm (stockinette)

Notions: clip on stitch marker *(or safety pin)*, scissors, tapestry needle, 30"/76 cm of 3/8"/.95 cm wide black velvet (or desired type) of ribbon, black thread *(or matching thread)*, sewing needle, three straight pins, measuring tape

Finished Size: 4.75" x 2.75"/12 cm tall x 7 cm wide, **1"**/2.5 cm deep (fits a standard tarot deck) *(unblocked)*

Directions

NOTE - *This bag is knit from the bottom up, beginning with a garter stitch bottom that is knitted flat. Stitches are then picked up along the perimeter of the bottom piece, continuing on to knit the lace pattern around the main body of the bag and finishing with a back flap, knitted flat. The ribbon is sewed on by hand (securing it to both sides of the bag) after the knitted bag is complete. Slipped stitches along the 4 edges give the bag some structure and an attractive appearance.*

1. Bottom:

CO **19 sts**, using the straight needles. Knit every row until the rectangle bottom piece measures **1"**/2.5 cm tall. *(approximately 10 rows)*

2. Body of Tarot Bag:

Beginning with the corner of a long side *(to your left)* and a short side *(to your right)*, pick up and knit **19 sts** along the LONG side with *n1*, **5 sts** on the SHORT side with *n2*, **19 sts** on the LONG side with *n3* and **5 sts** on the SHORT side with *n4*. You should have **48 sts total** on all the needles.

Place a clip-on st marker on one of the corner stitches at this point to denote the beginning of the round.

Knit **3** rounds.

For the next **47** rounds:

n1: (sl1, k1) on **odd** rows or (k2) on **even** rows, follow the **Shetland Fern Stitch** pattern for 15 sts, k2

n2: (sl1, k4) on **odd** rows of the pattern or (k5) on the **even** rows

n3: (sl1, k1) on **odd** rows or (k2) on **even** rows, follow the **Shetland Fern Stitch** pattern for 15 sts, k2

n4: (sl1, k4) on **odd** rows of the pattern or (k5) on the **even** rows

-----> On the **odd** rows, you are <u>slipping</u> the first stitch
On the **even** rows, you are <u>knitting</u> the first stitch

You will complete <u>2 full repeats</u> of the **Shetland Fern Stitch** pattern and <u>15 rounds</u> of the next repeat of the pattern.

3. Set up for the Front Flap *(fold-over section)***:**

On **Round 16** of the last repeat, stop **5** stitches before the end.

BO purlwise over the next **29 sts**. *(You will be binding off 5 sts from each side of the bag and 19 sts from the front of the bag.)* This will be the front of the tarot bag. Purl the next **18 sts**. You will have **19 sts** total on the needles. These stitches are the *fold-over* section for the flap of the bag.

You will now be working back and forth for the *fold-over* part of the flap:

Row 1: sl1, knit across all sts
Row 2: sl1, purl across all sts

Repeat Rows 1 & 2 (reverse stockinette) until *fold-over* measures **1"**/2.5 cm.

4. Front Flap of Tarot Bag:

Row 1: Sl1, p1, knit across to last 2 sts, p2
Row 2: Sl1, k1, purl across to last 2 sts, k2

Repeat Rows 1 & 2 until flap measures 4.5"/11.5 cm from *fold-over* section.

Next row: Sl1, purl to end
Final row: Sl1, knit to end

BO purlwise.

5. Adding ribbon:

At the halfway mark of the height and width of the back of the tarot bag, pin the center of the ribbon to this point *(with right side of ribbon facing you)*. Next, pin the ribbon on each edge of the bag *(at the slipped stitch sections)* bordering the back of the bag. (See **Figure A**) Using matching thread and sewing needle *(and making sure that the ribbon is smooth and flat against the back of the bag)*, sew the ribbon to the two edge sections only on the back of the bag. Remove all pins.

6. Finishing:

Weave in all ends. Slide your favorite tarot deck inside the bag, tie it up neatly and you're done! The flap of the tarot bag may be tucked in or left out.

Figure A

Shetland Fern Stitch: *(15 stitch pattern repeat)*

Round 1 *(rs)*: k7, yo, ssk, k6
Round 2 *(ws)* **and also Rounds 4, 6, 8 and 10:** knit
Round 3: k5, k2tog, yo, k1, yo, ssk, k5
Round 5: k4, k2tog, yo, k3, yo, ssk, k4
Round 7: k4, yo, ssk, yo, sk2p, yo, k2tog, yo, k4
Round 9: k2, k2tog, yo, k1, yo, ssk, k1, k2tog, yo, k1, yo, ssk, k2
Round 11: k2, (yo, ssk)2x, k3, (k2tog, yo)2x, k2
Round 12: k3, (yo, ssk)2x, k1, (k2tog, yo)2x, k3
Round 13: k4, yo, ssk, yo, sk2p, yo, k2tog, yo, k4
Round 14: k5, yo, ssk, k1, k2tog, yo, k5
Round 15: k6, yo, sk2p, yo, k6
Round 16: knit

Shetland Fern Stitch chart

	15	14	13	12	11	10	9	8	7	6	5	4	3	2	1	
																16
						O	3	\	O							15
					O	/			\	O						14
				O	/	O	3	\	O	\	O					13
		O	/	O	/					\	O	\	O			12
		O	/	O	/						\	O	\	O		11
																10
			\	O			O	/		\	O		O	/		9
																8
			O	/	O	\	O	\	O						7
																6
			\	O					O	/						5
																4
			\	O					O	/						3
																2
						\	O									1

Key

Knit — k (RS) Knit (WS) Purl		Purl 2 Together Tbl — p2tog tbl (RS) Purl 2 stitches together through back loop
K1 tbl — k1 tbl (RS) knit 1 stitch through back loop		Sl2 Kwise K1 Psso — s2kp (RS) slip 2 sts knitwise, k1, pass the slipped sts over
Knit 2 Together — k2tog (RS) Knit 2 stitches together		SK2P — sk2p (RS) Slip K2tog PSSO
Knit 3 Together — k3tog (RS) Knit 3 stitches together		Slip Knit Pass Over — skp (RS) Slip 1, knit 1, pass slipped stitch over
Knit 3 Together Tbl — k3tog tbl (RS) knit 3 stitches together through back loop		Slip With Yarn In Back — slip wyib (RS) yarn in back (WS) Slip stitch as if to purl, holding yarn in the front
Make One Knitwise — m1 (RS) Make one by lifting strand in between stitch just worked and the next stitch, knit into back of this thread		Slip Slip Knit — ssk (RS) slip, slip, knit slipped sts together
Make One Purlwise — m1p (RS) Make one by lifting strand in between stitch just worked and the next stitch, purl into back of this thread		No Stitch — x (RS) No Stitch (WS) No Stitch
Purl — p (RS) Purl (WS) Knit		Yarn Over — yo (RS) Yarn Over
Purl 2 Together — p2tog (RS) Purl 2 Together		

A Pattern for Understanding by Barbara Moore

(or…knitting can solve almost anything)

This adaptable pattern, er, *spread*, can work for a variety of questions. Use it for clarification and advice on any situation.

K: Knit

The Knit stitch is the fundamental building block of all knitting. The card in this position represents the foundation of the situation. Just as a competent knitter must understand both how to execute the knit stitch and its mechanics, you must understand this about your current question or situation.

P: Purl

The Purl stitch is the flipside of the Knit stitch. The card in this position shows an aspect of the situation that you haven't yet considered. Just as the Purl stitch adds variety and texture to knitting, this card provides insight into the complexity of your question or situation. Remember that many knitters admit that the Purl stitch not necessarily harder to execute yet it still interrupts their flow. This card may not feel smooth or easy to interpret. But stick with it. It'll be worth it.

Sl: Slip one stitch

Slipping one stitch means to slip one stitch without working it in any way. It is used as a decorative technique as well as a way of keeping knitting neat and tidy, particularly on edges. The card in this position is something you should just let slide. You may want to work it or change it, but just let it be. Later, you will see how it will prove either decorative or useful. For now, let it go.

YO: Yarn Over

Yarn Overs are a way of increasing knitting in a way that creates an airy, lacy effect. It is a way of adding yarn and space to a piece of work. The card in this position represents something that you should add to the situation to give you and others involved in the situation more space, more material to help fashion a lovely solution.

X: Frog!

Some knitters say that they are going to "frog" something when they mean they have to undo some stitches. The word "frog" is a play on the words "rip it" (ribbit!). Knitters frog things when a mistake has been made and there is no other way to correct the mistake. The card is this position is a mistake of some sort that you must correct in order to move toward a solution or resolution to the situation.

F: Finishing

Some knitters dread finishing, which means to completely assemble a piece by, for example, weaving in loose ends, attaching parts knitted separately, or grafting pieces together. The card in this position will help you clean up any loose ends and moving toward the final resolution.

B: Block

Blocking is usually the final step in a knitted project. It provides a polished and professional look by evening out and setting the stitches, removing wrinkles and any dirt accumulated during the knitting process, and making the final measurements accurate. Blocking usually involves water or steam, which cleans and relaxes the fibers so they can settle into play. This card is what you need to do as a final touch to set the situation into place. It can also involve a sense of cleansing or healing.

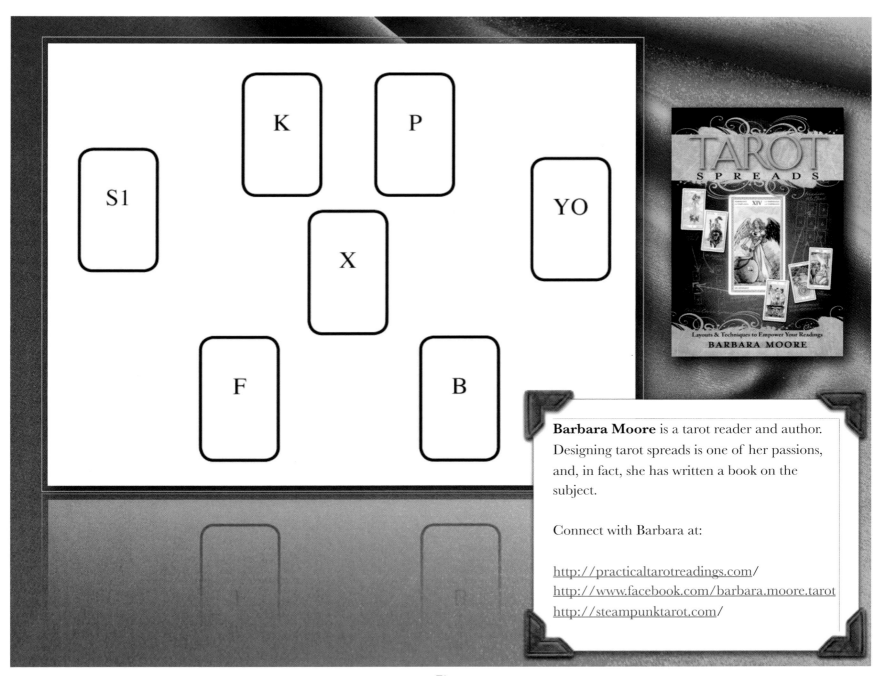

Barbara Moore is a tarot reader and author. Designing tarot spreads is one of her passions, and, in fact, she has written a book on the subject.

Connect with Barbara at:

http://practicaltarotreadings.com/
http://www.facebook.com/barbara.moore.tarot
http://steampunktarot.com/

Dreams of Alice Shawlette

This graceful and delicate shawlette was inspired by one of my favorite fairytale books, "*Alice's Adventures in Wonderland*" by Lewis Carroll. Although Alice isn't wrapped in a shawlette in the story, I always pictured her wearing one while sitting at the riverbank with her sister. This pattern is for a more experienced lace knitter, but could also be knit by an advanced beginner. If taken step by step, the lace patterns themselves aren't difficult. This small shawl would be a stunning accessory for a wedding or special occasion. "**Dreams of Alice**" is one of my favorite patterns in Wonderlace.

Pattern Difficulty:

Yarn:
(1) 1.76 oz/50 g skein (440 yds/402 m) of **Knit Picks** *Shimmer* (70% baby alpaca/30% silk) in "white #9437" AND
(1) 2 oz/58 g skein (825 yds/754.5 m) each of **Jade Sapphire** *Lacey Lamb* (100% superfine lambswool) in "turquoise #307" and "black #622"

Note: The center of the scarf uses **290 yds/265.2 m** or 1.16 oz/33 g of yarn, each of side lace panels uses **48 yds/43.9 m** or 0.6 oz/17 g (*96 yds/87.8 m or 1.2 oz/34 g total*) and **36 yards/32.9 m** or 0.09 oz/2.5 grams for each side final crocheted edge (*72 yards/65.8 m or 0.17 oz/5 g total*).

Needle: US **6** (4mm) 24-32"/61-81 cm circular or needle size necessary to obtain gauge

Gauge: **6** sts and **8** rows = 1"/2.5 cm (stockinette)

Hook: size **F** (4mm)

Notions: small stitch markers, scissors, tapestry needle, row counter, measuring tape, scrap lace weight yarn in a contrasting color (*optional, for lifelines*)

Finished Size: **42"** x **22"**//107 cm long x 56 cm wide (*blocked*)

Directions

1. Main Body of Shawlette:

Loosely CO **53** sts. (**REMEMBER:** Slip the first stitch of **every** row purlwise!)

Knit 1 row.
Purl 1 row.

Begin both patterns with **Row 1**.

Row 1 *(rs)*: sl1, follow the **Ladder Lace** pattern over 9 sts, PM, follow the **Pigtail Lace** pattern over the next 34 sts, PM, follow the **Ladder Lace** pattern over the last 9 sts, k1.

Row 2 *(ws)*: sl1, follow the **Ladder Lace** pattern over 9 sts, follow the **Pigtail Lace** pattern over the next 34 sts, follow the **Ladder Lace** pattern over the last 9 sts, k1. (*slipping st markers as you go*)

Repeat **Row 2** for the entire length of the main body - **150** repeats of the **Ladder Lace** pattern and **30** repeats of the **Pigtail Lace** pattern = **300 rows** total.

Knit 1 row.

BO loosely using the **K2togtbl Method** as follows: knit 1 st, *knit 1 st, move the st on RIGHT NEEDLE onto LEFT NEEDLE, k2togtbl*; repeat from *...* until every st is worked..

Cut yarn, leaving a 10"/25.4 cm tail, pull tail through the last st to secure. Shawlette at this point should measure approximately **36"/91.4 cm** long x **9"/22.8 cm** wide (*unblocked*).

2. Side Lace Borders: (You will be holding the laceweight yarn **DOUBLED**.)

Using the blue yarn *(or yarn colorway of your choice)* and with the RIGHT side of the shawlette facing you, pick up and knit **150 sts** along the entire length of the item - one in each of the slipped stitch openings.

On the next row, you will be <u>evenly decreasing 5 sts</u> along the row by purling 2 sts together every 28 sts: (p2tog, p28)5x. You will end with **145 sts.**

Follow the **Diamond Leaf Border** lace pattern for 1 full repeat - **27 rows**. BO loosely on WRONG side of the piece using the **K2togtbl Method** as follows: knit 1 st, *knit 1 st, move the st on RIGHT NEEDLE onto LEFT NEEDLE, k2togtbl*; repeat from *...* until every st is worked..

Cut yarn, leaving a **10"/25.4 cm** tail, pull tail through the last st to secure.

Repeat the **Lace Border** directions for the other side of the shawlette.

NOTE: The side lace borders should measure **3.75"/9.5 cm** in height after binding off.

3. Final Edge Borders: (You will be holding the laceweight yarn **DOUBLED**.)

Crochet Version, as pictured
Using the black yarn *(or yarn colorway of your choice)* and the crochet hook (with the RIGHT side of the shawlette facing you), slip stitch into the first bound off stitch on the right hand edge of the piece. Chain 3 sts. *Slip st into the next st, chain 3 sts*; repeat from *...* until every bound off stitch opening along the length of the shawlette is worked.

Cut yarn, leaving a **10"/25.4 cm** tail, pull tail through the last st to secure.

Optional Knitted Version
Using the black yarn *(or yarn colorway of your choice)* and knitting needle (with the RIGHT side of the shawlette facing you), pick up and knit into every bound off stitch opening along the entire length of the shawlette. Next 2 rows: purl across entire round. BO loosely using the **K2togtbl Method:** knit 1 st, *knit 1 st, move the st on RIGHT NEEDLE onto LEFT NEEDLE, k2togtbl*; repeat from *...* until every st is worked.

Cut yarn, leaving a **10"/25.4 cm** tail, pull tail through the last st to secure.

Repeat the **Final Edge Border** directions of your choice for the other side of the shawlette.

4. Finishing:

Weave in all ends, neatly. To **block the shawlette**, soak the shawl in a sink *(or small washtub)* full of tepid water with a no-rinse wool wash for at least 30 minutes. Gently remove item from the water, lightly squeeze out the excess water and roll in a towel, pressing firmly. *(You can also place the item in a lingerie bag and put on the spin only cycle of your washing machine.)*

Using blocking boards, foam boards, a thick carpet or your bed lay out the shawlette - right side up. Use blocking pins to pin the item out to suggested (or desired) dimensions, making sure to pin the tips of the diamond leaves out dramatically, or as an alternate suggestion, pin out each of the crocheted loops. Try to stretch the lace enough to open it up nicely, but not enough to snap the yarn. Let block for several hours until dry or, ideally, overnight.

Ladder Lace: *(9 stitch repeat)*

Row 1 *(rs)*: k1, skp, yo(2x), s2kp, yo(2x), k2tog, k1
Row 2 *(ws)*: (p2, k1)2x, p3

Repeat Rows 1 & 2 for pattern.

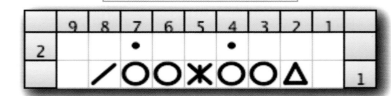

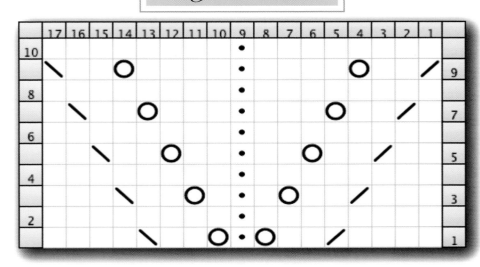

Pigtail Lace: *(17 stitch repeat)*

Row 1 *(rs)*: k4, k2tog, k2, yo, p1, yo, k2, ssk, k4
Row 2 *(ws)*: p8, k1, p8
Row 3: k3, k2tog, k2, yo, k1, p1, k1, yo, k2, ssk, k3
Row 5: k2, k2tog, k2, yo, k2, p1, k2, yo, k2, ssk, k2
Row 7: k1, k2tog, k2, yo, k3, p1, k3, yo, k2, ssk, k1
Row 9: k2tog, k2, yo, k4, p1, k4, yo, k2, ssk
Row 10: repeat Row 2.

Repeat Rows 1-10 for pattern.

Key

☐	Knit k (RS) Knit (WS) Purl	⃗	Purl 2 Together Tbl p2tog tbl (RS) Purl 2 stitches together through back loop
⅄	K1 tbl k1 tbl (RS) knit 1 stitch through back loop	⋉	Sl2 Kwise K1 Psso s2kp (RS) slip 2 sts knitwise, k1, pass the slipped sts over
╱	Knit 2 Together k2tog (RS) Knit 2 stitches together	ᴈ	SK2P sk2p (RS) Slip K2tog PSSO
⋏	Knit 3 Together k3tog (RS) Knit 3 stitches together	△	Slip Knit Pass Over skp (RS) Slip 1, knit 1, pass slipped stitch over
⋋	Knit 3 Together Tbl k3tog tbl (RS) knit 3 stitches together through back loop	⋁	Slip With Yarn In Back slip wyib (RS) yarn in back (WS) Slip stitch as if to purl, holding yarn in the front
Ⓜ	Make One Knitwise m1 (RS) Make one by lifting strand in between stitch just worked and the next stitch, knit into back of this thread	╲	Slip Slip Knit ssk (RS) slip, slip, knit slipped sts together
Ⓜ	Make One Purlwise m1p (RS) Make one by lifting strand in between stitch just worked and the next stitch, purl into back of this thread	■	No Stitch x (RS) No Stitch (WS) No Stitch
•	Purl p (RS) Purl (WS) Knit	Ⓞ	Yarn Over yo (RS) Yarn Over
⃒	Purl 2 Together p2tog (RS) Purl 2 Together		

Diamond Leaf Border

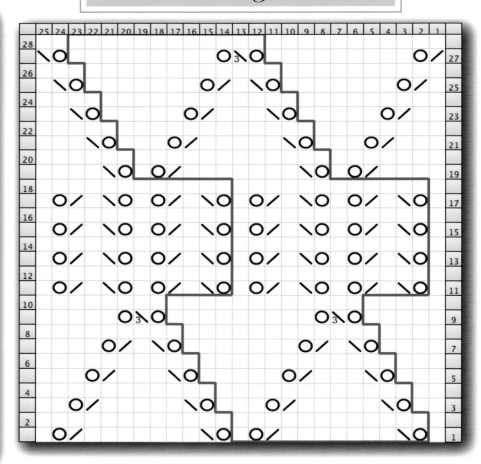

Repeat pattern in **BLUE.**

76

<u>Diamond Leaf Border</u>: *(12 st + 1 stitch repeat)*

Row 1 *(rs)*: k1, *yo, ssk, k7, k2tog, yo, k1*; repeat *...* to end
Row 2 *(ws)* **and all even rows:** purl across
Row 3: k2, *yo, ssk, k5, k2tog, yo, k3*; repeat *...* ending with a k2 in the last repeat
Row 5: k3, *yo, ssk, k3, k2tog, yo, k5*; repeat *...* ending with a k3 in the last repeat
Row 7: k4, *yo, ssk, k1, k2tog, yo, k7*; repeat *...* ending with a k4 in the last repeat
Row 9: k5, *yo, sk2p, yo, k9*; repeat *...* ending with a k5 in the last repeat
Row 11, 13, 15, 17: k1, *yo, ssk, k1, k2tog, yo, k1*; repeat *...* to end
Row 19: k4, k2tog, yo, k1, *yo, ssk, k7, k2tog, yo, k1*; repeat *...* to last 6 sts, yo ssk, k4
Row 21: k3, k2tog, yo, k3, *yo, ssk, k5, k2tog, yo, k3*; repeat *...* to last 5 sts, yo, ssk, k3
Row 23: k2, k2tog, yo, k5, *yo, ssk, k3, k2tog, yo, k5*; repeat *...* to last 4 sts, yo, ssk, k2
Row 25: k1, k2tog, yo, k7, *yo, ssk, k1, k2tog, yo, k7*; repeat *...* to last 3 sts, yo, ssk, k1
Row 27: k2tog, yo, k9, *yo, sk2p, yo, k9*; repeat *...* to last 2 sts, yo, ssk
Row 28: purl

Repeat Rows 1-28 for pattern. This border pattern will only be worked for one **full** repeat.

Gina House

is an archer, a knitter, a reader, a tarot card and book lover.
She is an instructor of yoga, hula hooping/hoopdance, archery, knitting;
a mom of two video game savvy boys and has a loving, supportive hubby.
She loves journals, Agatha Christie books and luxurious yarns.
She is short, busty, talks too much, smiles a lot, shares too much information
and sneezes incredibly loudly at times.
Green beans make her happy and mushrooms make her sad.
Someday, she will publish a children's book.
In the meantime,
she will have to settle for
pink cupcakes, silver glitter and sparkly tiaras.

To find out more about Gina, visit her website at http://www.ginahouse.net

Looking for a fun, FREE knitting app?

❋ Free patterns with preview pictures, skill difficulty and yarn weight
❋ Yarn Gauge Chart
❋ 5 In app pattern/book purchases
❋ Useful knitting blog posts
❋ Search for patterns by skill difficulty, yarn weight and yarn company
❋ Knitting Podcast
❋ Ability to download free patterns from your portable device to your
   computer
❋ Helpful links
❋ Frequently Asked Question (FAQ) section
❋ Beautiful, full color photographs of designs from "Dreamscape"
   and "Wonderlace"
❋ Knitting tutorials
❋ Option of purchasing "Sleepy Eyes Knits: Dreamscape" (available now!) and
   "Sleepy Eyes Knits: Wonderlace" books directly to your device
              (COMING SOON!)

Acknowledgements

My Beautiful Knitwear Models

Jacqueline Wolk (Queen's Mirror Shawl, Loralee Cowl, Violet's Garden Socks)

Heather Horton (Dreams of Alice Shawlette)

Hilary Murphy (Beauty Shawl)

Emma Fontaine (Veronica Earrings)

Aimee Huntemann (Poison Apple Beret)

Hanna Foley (Megaera Mitts)

Kate Carlton (Taylor Cowl)

Michael Mitchell (Hunter Scarf)

Amazing Test Knitters and Pattern Editors:

Aimee Huntemann (primary editor), Sarah Selli, Heather Horton, Jacqueline Wolk, Valerie Kelley,

Jessica Ostrow, Jeannine Russell, Judith Beckman, Elizabeth Caplice, Lora Kinberger, Nancy Tella

Also many thanks to:

Barbara Moore & Llewellyn Worldwide for use of the fantastic Steampunk Tarot deck (http://www.llewellyn.com)

Pixlr-o-matic (Autodesk) for use of their awesome photo editing software (http://pixlr.com/o-matic)

Angela Rogers Marshall for creating Dreamscape & Wonderlace scents in her amazing Poison Apple Apothecary

products! (http://poisonappleapothecary.com)

To those who mean so much...

To my husband, Ian - who encouraged me, supported me and gave me countless hours of computer help throughout this 2 year process. I love you!

To my sons, Tim and Ben - who make me proud and make me laugh every single day. I am so lucky and I love you both!

To my parents, Thomas & Karen; my sister, Kim and my grandmother, Catherine, for their love and faith in me through all of my creative ventures. Love you!

funded with

KICK STARTER

Kickstarter Backers!

Words cannot express the gratitude that I feel to everyone who donated to my Kickstarter project. Thank you from the bottom of my heart and I couldn't have done it without any of you!!!!

Chip Marshall
Jaimie & Anthony Gabrielson
Angelina Milinazzo
Karen & Thomas Chin
Ian House
Sandi Oswalt
Abbie Davis
Edith House
Kerry Pinkham Murphy
Richard Rouse
Bethany Kim Cecere
Julia Kubik
Mary Marshall
Beth Doan
Pen Reyes
Felice House
Rebecca Richkus
Peta Richkus
Heather Horton
David Weaver
Laurin Marden
Sarah Taylor Selli
Chris Haddad
Jacqueline Wolk
Caitlin Doran
Tyler Hall
Rose Robinson
Amy Wilson
Liz Xu Wilson
H Lynnea
Amanda Hosmer
Delia Dubois
Melissa Whittemore
Christy Schakhart
Sarah McCusker
Kiki Hall
JessaLu Meyer
Ulrike Meilke
Becca Fletcher
Shael Hawman
Emily Ringelman
Victoria Blum Mothes
John Shappy *(first backer!)*
Aimee & Neil Huntemann
DW